MW00931830

STRANGE BUT TRUE FISHING FACTS

Curiosities and Stories

1

The Great White Shark of 1986.

Frank Mundus, a legendary fisherman, earned much of his fame thanks to his capture of a giant great white shark in 1986.

This event took place near Montauk, New York, an area known for its abundance of marine life and its popularity among sport fishermen.

The great white shark caught by Mundus weighed 3,427 pounds (1,558 kg), making it one of the largest great white sharks ever recorded.

He used rod and reel fishing techniques, highlighting his skill as a fisherman and the quality of his equipment.

This feat solidified Mundus's reputation as one of the best shark fishermen in the world, attracting global attention.

Frank Mundus is widely considered to be the inspiration for the character Quint in Peter Benchley's novel "Jaws" and its film adaptation directed by Steven Spielberg.

Although Benchley did not officially confirm that Quint was based on Mundus, the similarities in their personalities and fishing methods are notable.

Mundus was known for his straightforward style and innovative approach to shark fishing, often using live bait and, in his early years, even dead horses as bait to attract large sharks.

Mundus is considered a pioneer in the fishing of large sharks, revolutionizing the techniques and tactics used in catching these predators.

Later in his life, he became an advocate for shark conservation, promoting catch and release to protect shark populations.

He wrote several books on shark fishing and appeared on numerous television programs, sharing his knowledge and experiences with a wider audience.

He conducted his expeditions aboard his boat called "Cricket II," which became an icon due to the numerous feats and catches recorded from it.

Thanks to Mundus, Montauk became a pilgrimage destination for shark fishing enthusiasts, attracting fishermen from all over the world.

The story of Frank Mundus and his capture of the great white shark in 1986 remains one of the most impressive in the history of sport fishing, and his legacy endures both in popular culture and modern shark conservation practices.

2

The Giant Catfish of Thailand.

In 2005, local fishermen in the Mekong River, Thailand, caught a giant catfish weighing around 646 pounds (293 kg).

This fish, known as the Mekong giant catfish (Pangasianodon gigas), is one of the largest freshwater fish species in the world.

Its capture was notable both for its size and the effort required to pull it from the water.

The Mekong giant catfish is native to the Mekong basin, which spans several Southeast Asian countries, including Thailand, Laos, Cambodia, and Vietnam.

The species is classified as critically endangered due to factors such as overfishing, dam construction that alters its habitat, and water pollution.

The capture of this giant catfish brought international attention to the need to protect this species and its habitat, highlighting the high biodiversity of the Mekong River.

The river is known for hosting numerous fish species, many of which are endemic to this region.

The existence of fish of this size underscores the ecological importance of the Mekong and the need for sustainable conservation efforts.

Scientists and conservationists have used the capture of this specimen to advocate for stricter fishing policies and the protection of the river's habitat.

In addition to its ecological importance, the Mekong giant catfish holds significant cultural value for local communities that have depended on this and other fish for their subsistence for generations.

3

The Giant Bluefin Tuna of Ken Fraser.

In 1979, Ken Fraser caught a giant bluefin tuna weighing 1,496 pounds (679 kg) in the waters of Nova Scotia, Canada.

This impressive bluefin tuna, known for its massive size, remains the largest ever recorded in the history of sport fishing.

Catching this tuna was no easy task; Ken Fraser had to fight for 45 minutes to land it, demonstrating not only the fish's strength but also the skill and endurance of the fisherman.

This event highlighted the richness of the waters of Nova Scotia, known for being a favorable habitat for bluefin tuna due to their nutrient-rich currents.

The bluefin tuna (Thunnus thynnus) is a highly valued species both for its size and its quality as a fish, especially in markets like Japan where tuna is used for sushi and sashimi.

Bluefin tuna can swim at high speeds and migrate long distances, making them an exciting challenge for sport fishermen.

Ken Fraser's catch not only earned him a place in world records but also increased attention on bluefin tuna fishing in Nova Scotia, attracting fishermen from around the world.

This feat has been widely documented and celebrated in the sport fishing community, serving as a testament to the possibility of catching large fish with the right techniques and determination.

4

The Goliath Tigerfish of Jeremy Wade.

Jeremy Wade, known for his television show "River Monsters," captured a goliath tigerfish in the Congo River in 2010.

This fish, famous for its sharp teeth and aggressive nature, weighed 110 pounds (50 kg) and is considered one of the most dangerous fish to catch.

The goliath tigerfish (Hydrocynus goliath) is known for its imposing teeth, which can measure several centimeters long, and its reputation as a fierce predator in its natural habitat.

Jeremy Wade, a British biologist and extreme angler, has explored many of the world's most dangerous waters in search of creatures that defy imagination.

His capture of the goliath tigerfish was one of the highlights of his series, showcasing not only the intense struggle these fish can put up but also the inherent danger in trying to catch them.

Goliath tigerfish are primarily found in the Congo River basin and are known for attacking other fish and occasionally humans, contributing to their feared reputation.

The capture of this fish was a significant challenge for Wade, requiring not only skill and fishing experience but also a deep understanding of the dangers present in the Congo River environment.

Wade's success in capturing a goliath tigerfish of such size and power underscores his exceptional ability as an angler and his dedication to discovering and documenting some of the world's most extraordinary fish species.

The goliath tigerfish is not only an impressive sight due to its size and ferocity, but it also highlights the rich biodiversity of the Congo River, one of Africa's most important river systems.

This river is home to an incredible variety of species, many of which are unique to this region.

Wade's capture helped raise awareness about these fish and the need to conserve their natural habitats to maintain ecological balance in these waters.

The popularity of the show "River Monsters" and Jeremy Wade's adventures have inspired many to take an interest in sport fishing and marine biology, as well as to appreciate the importance of conserving aquatic ecosystems.

5

The Giant Squid of Tsunemi Kubodera.

In 2012, researcher and fisherman Tsunemi Kubodera achieved an impressive feat by filming and capturing a giant squid in the depths of the Pacific Ocean.

This squid, which measured over 26 feet (8 meters) in length, is known as one of the first to be captured on video in its natural habitat, representing a significant breakthrough in the study of these enigmatic marine creatures.

The giant squid (Architeuthis dux) has long been the subject of myths and legends due to its colossal size and elusiveness.

The capture and filming of this giant squid by Tsunemi Kubodera was a remarkable achievement in the field of marine biology.

Using special cameras and equipment prepared for the extreme depths of the ocean, Kubodera and his team were able to document for the first time the behavior of a giant squid in its natural environment.

This documentation provided valuable information on how these animals hunt and move in the ocean depths, areas that are difficult to explore due to extreme pressure and darkness.

Kubodera's giant squid was captured in the Japan Trench, a region known for its marine biodiversity and the great depths of the ocean.

The filming and capture not only demonstrated the existence of these giants in the ocean depths but also challenged many previous perceptions about their behavior and ecology.

The length of the squid, exceeding 26 feet, and its imposing presence in the captured footage, underscored the magnificence of these creatures.

Before this achievement, most sightings of giant squids were based on carcasses found floating on the ocean surface or stranded on shores.

The filming in its natural habitat represented a milestone, as it allowed scientists to observe a live, active giant squid in its environment, offering an unprecedented view of its life and habits.

Tsunemi Kubodera's work has been fundamental in increasing our understanding of giant squids and has inspired other researchers to continue exploring the ocean depths.

His contribution to scientific knowledge has helped demystify these impressive creatures and has opened new avenues of research into the mysteries that still persist in the ocean depths.

The story of this giant squid is not only a testament to technological advancement and perseverance in scientific exploration but also a reminder of how little we still know about the oceans and the creatures that inhabit them.

6

George Perry's Largemouth Bass.

In 1932, George Perry caught a 22-pound, 4-ounce (10.1 kg) largemouth bass in Montgomery Lake, Georgia.

This world record bass has stood the test of time and remains one of the most legendary stories in freshwater fishing.

George Perry's catch occurred during the Great Depression, a period when fishing was not only a pastime but also a means of subsistence.

Perry, a farmer and amateur fisherman, was fishing for food when he managed to catch the record-breaking bass.

At that time, fishing methods and equipment were much more rudimentary than today, making his achievement even more impressive.

George Perry caught the bass using basic fishing gear, and it is known that he was fishing from a small cypress boat, along with his friend Jack Page.

The two men were fishing in Montgomery Lake, taking advantage of a day off from farm work.

To catch the bass, Perry used a simple fishing rod and a baitcasting reel.

The choice of bait was crucial to his success, as Perry used an artificial lure called the "Creek Chub Fintail Shiner," which was a popular lure at that time.

This lure was designed to mimic a small fish, an attractive target for a large bass.

The "Creek Chub Fintail Shiner" was a surface lure that mimicked the movement of an injured fish, provoking the bass to attack.

Perry cast the lure near a structure in the water, likely a submerged log or vegetation, places where large bass typically lurk to ambush their prey.

When the bass bit the lure, Perry immediately realized he had caught something extraordinary.

The fight to bring the fish out of the water was intense, but Perry, with his experience and determination, managed to bring the bass aboard the small boat.

After the catch, Perry and Page took the fish to a local store where it was weighed on a certified scale, confirming its weight of 22 pounds and 4 ounces.

The catch was reported to a fishing magazine, which verified the measurements and awarded Perry the world record.

Perry's catch not only earned him a place in the world records but also increased attention on bass fishing in Montgomery Lake and other parts of the United States.

This achievement has been widely documented and celebrated in the sport fishing community, serving as a testament to what is possible with skill, patience, and the right choice of gear and bait.

Perry's record has inspired generations of anglers, who see in him an example of what is possible with dedication and a passion for fishing.

Over the years, there have been reports of bass that might have surpassed Perry's record, but none have been officially verified and accepted by the International Game Fish Association (IGFA).

7

The Giant Grouper of Ernest Hemingway.

The famous writer and avid fisherman Ernest Hemingway caught a 500-pound (227 kg) grouper off the coast of Cuba in the 1930s.

Hemingway was known for his passion for deep-sea fishing, and this was one of his most notable trophies, reflecting his skill and dedication to the sport.

Hemingway often conducted his fishing expeditions on his boat called "Pilar," a sport fishing yacht he acquired in 1934.

This boat was equipped with the latest fishing technology of the time, including rods and reels designed to withstand the strength of large deep-sea fish.

To capture the enormous grouper, Hemingway used robust bottom fishing gear.

This involved a strong fishing rod and a large reel capable of storing a heavy-duty fishing line, capable of withstanding the tremendous struggle of a fish of this size.

The choice of bait to capture the giant grouper was crucial.

Hemingway used live bait, which is a common and effective technique for attracting large groupers.

In this case, the bait likely consisted of small to medium-sized fish, such as sardines or jacks, which are attractive to groupers due to their natural movement in the water.

Hemingway placed the bait on a large, strong hook designed to catch and hold large fish.

He then dropped the line to the sea floor, where groupers typically inhabit near underwater structures such as coral reefs, shipwrecks, or rocky formations.

Once the grouper bit the hook, an intense struggle ensued.

Groupers are known for their strength and resistance, and the battle to pull a 500-pound fish out of the water was monumental.

Hemingway, with his vast experience and physical strength, fought the fish, using leverage techniques and patience to wear down the grouper before finally bringing it to the surface.

This achievement not only demonstrated Hemingway's skill as a fisherman but also his passion and dedication to the sport.

Catching a grouper of this size required not only the right equipment but also a deep understanding of the fish's behavior and impeccable technique.

Hemingway's capture of this giant grouper is one of many stories that contribute to his legend as both a fisherman and a writer.

Hemingway, who lived in Cuba for many years, had a deep connection with the sea and fishing, which was reflected in his literary work, especially in "The Old Man and the Sea," a novel that won the Pulitzer Prize and the Nobel Prize in Literature.

8

The Giant Piranha of Thomas Peschak.

In 2012, photographer and fisherman Thomas Peschak caught a giant piranha weighing 13 pounds (6 kg) in the Amazon.

Although not as large compared to other fish on this list, the piranha is famous for its ferocity, and the catch was notable for its rarity and the associated danger.

To capture the giant piranha, Thomas Peschak used specific fishing techniques for aggressive and carnivorous species like the piranha.

Peschak, known for his work as a wildlife photographer and his skills in sport fishing, was well-prepared to face the challenge of catching a large piranha.

Peschak employed a strong and flexible fishing rod, combined with a robust reel capable of handling the strength and resistance of a piranha.

The fishing line used was high-strength, capable of withstanding the sharp teeth of the piranha and the sudden pulls during the struggle.

The choice of bait was crucial to attracting a giant piranha. Peschak used fresh bait, which is highly effective in attracting piranhas due to their scavenging and carnivorous instincts.

In this case, the bait consisted of fish chunks, which emitted a strong and attractive smell for piranhas in the Amazon waters.

Once the piranha bit the hook, an intense battle began.

Piranhas, despite their relatively small size, are known for their strength and their ability to fight vigorously when hooked.

The giant piranha caught by Peschak was no exception, offering fierce resistance.

Peschak had to use his experience and skill to manage the rod and reel, applying constant pressure to tire out the piranha without breaking the line.

The struggle was intense, but eventually, Peschak managed to bring the 13-pound piranha to the surface, securing his catch.

The capture of this giant piranha by Thomas Peschak was significant not only because of the size of the fish but also because of the rarity and danger associated with piranha fishing in the Amazon.

Piranhas are known for their sharp teeth and aggressive behavior, making their capture an exciting and risky challenge.

Peschak, as a photographer and conservationist, took the opportunity to document the biodiversity of the Amazon and highlight the importance of conserving these unique ecosystems.

His capture of the giant piranha was widely documented and helped raise awareness about the rich wildlife of the Amazon and the challenges of preserving it.

9

The Beluga Sturgeon of Joerg Dachwitz.

In 2007, German fisherman Joerg Dachwitz caught a beluga sturgeon weighing 2,386 pounds (1,082 kg) in the Volga River, Russia.

This enormous fish, measuring over 18 feet (5.5 meters), was one of the most impressive catches in the history of sturgeon fishing.

To catch a beluga sturgeon of this size, Joerg Dachwitz used specialized deep-water fishing techniques, adapted to face the resistance and strength of one of the largest freshwater fish.

The beluga sturgeon is known not only for its colossal size but also for its formidable fight when hooked.

Dachwitz employed a high-strength fishing rod and a robust reel, specifically designed for fishing large fish.

The fishing line used was of a very strong gauge to withstand the weight and power of the beluga sturgeon.

This specialized equipment is crucial to ensure that the line does not break during the intense struggle that follows the hooking of a fish of this magnitude.

The choice of bait is vital to attract a beluga sturgeon.

Dachwitz used natural bait, which generally consists of small fish, worms, or chunks of fish, that are especially effective in attracting these large predators.

In this case, the bait was likely placed near the bottom of the river, where sturgeons typically forage for food.

Once the beluga sturgeon bit the hook, a monumental struggle began.

Sturgeons are known for their endurance and ability to engage in long, exhausting battles.

Dachwitz had to employ all his skills and experience to manage the rod and reel, applying constant but careful pressure to tire the fish without breaking the line.

Catching a fish of this size requires not only strength and patience but also a deep understanding of the fish's behavior and the river's dynamics.

The fight lasted several hours, during which the sturgeon repeatedly attempted to escape into the depths of the Volga River.

Finally, after an exhausting battle, Dachwitz managed to bring the beluga sturgeon to the surface.

With the help of his team, they were able to secure and measure the colossal fish, confirming its impressive size of 2,386 pounds and over 18 feet in length.

10

Sean Konrad's Rainbow Trout.

In 2009, Sean Konrad caught a 48-pound (21.77 kg) rainbow trout in Lake Diefenbaker, Saskatchewan, Canada.

This world record surpassed the previous record set by his twin brother, Adam Konrad, making the story even more intriguing.

To capture this record-breaking rainbow trout, Sean Konrad used specific trout fishing techniques, adapted to catch large fish in Lake Diefenbaker.

Trout fishing requires a combination of skill, knowledge of the environment, and the proper selection of equipment and bait.

Sean employed a high-strength fishing rod and a reel designed to handle large fish.

The line used was made of a strong and durable material, capable of withstanding the weight and struggle of such a large rainbow trout.

When fishing for trout of this size, it's crucial to have equipment that can endure the intense fight these fish offer.

The choice of bait was essential to attract a trout of this size.

Sean used artificial bait specific to trout, which likely included large lures and imitations of small fish or aquatic invertebrates, which are part of the natural diet of trout in the lake.

The lures used had to be attractive and capable of triggering the predatory instinct of a large rainbow trout.

When the rainbow trout bit the hook, an exciting and intense battle began.

Rainbow trout are known for their strength and ability to perform acrobatic jumps and fast runs, making their capture an exhilarating challenge for any angler.

Sean had to use all his skills and experience to manage the rod and reel, maintaining constant and controlled pressure to prevent the fish from escaping or breaking the line.

The fight with the rainbow trout was demanding and prolonged, requiring patience and technique to tire the fish without losing it.

After an exhausting battle, Sean finally managed to bring the enormous trout to the surface, confirming its impressive size and weight.

Sean Konrad's capture of this 48-pound rainbow trout not only set a new world record but also added a fascinating element to the story due to the friendly rivalry with his twin brother, Adam Konrad, who previously held the record.

This dynamic between the Konrad brothers drew the attention of the fishing community and the media, highlighting their exceptional skill and dedication to sport fishing.

Lake Diefenbaker, where the catch was made, is known for hosting large trout due to its favorable environment and the quality of its waters.

11

The Giant Sunfish of Karl Schmidt.

In 1908, Karl Schmidt caught a sunfish (Mola mola) that weighed approximately 3,500 pounds (1,600 kg) off the coast of Santa Catalina, California.

This fish is one of the largest bony fish in the world, and its capture was a significant event due to its size and unusual shape.

To catch the enormous sunfish, Karl Schmidt used deep-sea fishing techniques adapted to the unique characteristics of this fish.

Fishing for sunfish requires patience and robust equipment, given the immense mass and resistance of these fish.

Schmidt employed a strong and flexible fishing rod, suitable for deep-sea fishing and capable of withstanding the weight and struggle of a large fish.

The reel used was designed to handle long stretches of line and offer high resistance, crucial to prevent the fish from breaking the line during the capture.

The fishing line was high-strength, probably made of a material like Dacron or braided wire, capable of enduring the tension of dragging a 3,500-pound fish.

The hook used would have been large and robust, suitable for firmly hooking into the mouth of the sunfish.

The choice of bait was essential to attract the sunfish, so Schmidt used live bait, an effective technique for attracting large oceanic fish.

The bait consisted of squid and small fish, which are part of the natural diet of the sunfish.

These live baits were presented in a way that made them move naturally in the water, attracting the attention of the sunfish.

When the sunfish bit the hook, an intense battle began.

Sunfish, although not known for their speed, are extremely strong and can offer considerable resistance due to their large size and body shape.

Schmidt had to use all his skills and experience to manage the rod and reel, applying constant and controlled pressure to prevent the fish from escaping or breaking the line.

The struggle lasted several hours, during which the sunfish repeatedly tried to dive into the depths of the ocean.

The fish's resistance and weight made this one of the most challenging and exhausting catches.

Finally, after an exhausting battle, Schmidt and his team managed to bring the sunfish to the surface and secure it.

12

Max Muggeridge's Hammerhead Shark.

In 2006, Max Muggeridge, an Australian fisherman, caught a 14-foot (4.3 meters) hammerhead shark off the coast of Australia.

The catch was notable not only for the size of the shark but also because it was made from the shore rather than a boat.

Catching a hammerhead shark of this size from the shore requires a combination of advanced skills, specialized equipment, and a careful strategy.

Max Muggeridge used beach fishing techniques adapted to handle the strength and resistance of such a large shark.

To capture the hammerhead shark, Muggeridge employed an extremely sturdy fishing rod and a high-capacity reel, suitable for shore fishing for large sharks.

The equipment needed to withstand the tremendous pressure and resistance that a shark of this size can exert during the fight.

The fishing line used was high-strength, likely made of materials like monofilament or braided line, capable of enduring strong currents and the abrasion caused by the shark's rough skin.

The hook used was large and high-quality, designed to securely latch into the shark's mouth and withstand its powerful bite.

The choice of bait was crucial to attract the hammerhead shark.

Muggeridge used fresh and bloody bait, which is highly effective in attracting sharks due to their keen sense of smell.

The bait consisted of large chunks of fish and squid, which are attractive to sharks.

To maximize the effectiveness of the bait, Muggeridge placed it on a large hook and cast it as far out into the water as possible.

Often, techniques like "kayak baiting" are used, where the bait is taken offshore with the help of a kayak. However, in this case, being from the shore, the technique involved powerful and precise casting.

When the hammerhead shark bit the hook, an intense and prolonged battle began.

Hammerhead sharks are known for their strength and agility, and this 14-foot specimen was no exception.

The fight involved multiple runs out to sea, sudden tugs, and considerable skill from Muggeridge to keep the line taut and prevent the shark from escaping.

The struggle lasted several hours, during which Muggeridge had to use all his skills and endurance to control the shark.

Catching from the shore presents unique challenges, as the fisherman must handle both the equipment and the terrain and wave conditions.

Finally, after an exhausting battle, Muggeridge managed to bring the hammerhead shark to the shore.

The catch was secured with the help of other fishermen and onlookers, who helped measure and document the shark's impressive size before releasing it back into the sea.

13

The Giant Tuna of Prince Albert I of Monaco.

In 1885, Prince Albert I of Monaco caught a giant bluefin tuna weighing 850 pounds (386 kg) in the Mediterranean Sea.

This catch was notable not only for the size of the fish but also because Prince Albert was a renowned oceanographer and advocate for marine conservation.

Catching a bluefin tuna of this size in the 19th century required advanced fishing techniques for the time and a deep understanding of bluefin tuna behavior.

Prince Albert I, with his experience in marine studies and his passion for fishing, used methods that combined traditional skills with his scientific knowledge.

To capture the giant bluefin tuna, Prince Albert I used a sturdy fishing rod and a large, durable reel, suitable for handling the tremendous strength and speed of the bluefin tuna.

The equipment was designed to withstand long battles, which are common in the fishing of large tuna, known for their fast and powerful runs.

The fishing line used was made of a strong and resilient material, probably hemp or braided cotton, which were common materials in fishing at the time.

This line needed to withstand the tension exerted by an 850-pound fish.

The choice of bait was crucial to attracting the bluefin tuna.

Prince Albert I used natural bait, small fish, and squid, which are part of the natural diet of bluefin tuna.

These baits were presented in a way that made them move attractively in the water, simulating the natural prey of the tuna.

The live or fresh bait was cast into the water and left at an appropriate depth where tunas usually hunt.

The patience and knowledge of Prince Albert about the feeding habits of the bluefin tuna played a crucial role in attracting a fish of this size.

When the bluefin tuna bit the hook, an epic battle began, as bluefin tunas are known for their speed and endurance, and this 850-pound specimen was no exception.

The fight was intense and prolonged, with the tuna making several long and powerful runs to try to break free.

Prince Albert I had to use all his skills and experience to manage the rod and reel, applying constant and controlled pressure to tire the fish without breaking the line.

Catching the fish from a boat in the Mediterranean added a level of difficulty, as the sea can be unpredictable and conditions can change.

Finally, after a long and exhausting struggle, Prince Albert I and his team managed to bring the bluefin tuna aboard the boat.

The catch was a triumph not only because of the size of the fish but also due to the skill and patience demonstrated during the battle.

The capture of this giant bluefin tuna by Prince Albert I of Monaco in 1885 is a notable story in the history of sport fishing.

This achievement reflected not only the Prince's prowess as a fisherman but also his deep knowledge of the sea and its life.

13

The Giant Stingray of the Chao Phraya River.

In 2009, Ian Welch, a British marine biologist, caught a giant stingray in the Chao Phraya River, Thailand.

The stingray measured 14 feet (4.2 meters) and weighed over 550 pounds (250 kg).

This species is known for its size and strength, and the capture required the coordinated effort of several fishermen.

Catching a giant stingray of this size in a river like the Chao Phraya presents unique challenges due to the fish's strength and endurance, as well as the river conditions.

Ian Welch used fishing techniques adapted to handle these large and powerful fish.

To capture the giant stingray, Welch employed an extremely sturdy fishing rod and a high-capacity reel, designed to withstand the tremendous strength of a stingray of this size.

The equipment had to be able to handle not only the weight of the fish but also the strong currents of the river.

The fishing line used was made of a very strong material, probably high-quality braid, capable of withstanding the extreme tension during the battle with the stingray.

Additionally, the hook used was large and strong, suitable for securely latching into the stingray's mouth without coming loose during the struggle.

The choice of bait was crucial to attract the giant stingray, as Welch used live bait, such as small fish and chunks of fish, which are part of the natural diet of stingrays.

These live baits were presented in a way that made them move naturally in the water, attracting the stingray's attention.

To maximize the effectiveness of the bait, Welch and his team placed the bait in areas of the river where stingrays typically forage, leveraging their knowledge of the behavior and feeding habits of these fish.

When the giant stingray bit the hook, an intense and prolonged battle began.

Stingrays are known for their incredible strength and ability to make powerful dives towards the riverbed.

The fight required not only Welch's skill and endurance but also the coordination of his team.

The battle lasted 3 hours, during which Welch and his team had to apply constant and controlled pressure to tire the stingray without breaking the line.

Catching from the shore of the Chao Phraya River presented additional challenges, as the terrain and river currents could complicate the handling of the rod and reel.

Finally, after an exhausting battle, Welch and his team managed to bring the giant stingray to the shore.

The catch was secured with the help of several fishermen, who worked together to measure and document the impressive size of the stingray before releasing it back into the river.

14

The Paddlefish of the Yangtze River.

In 2007, Chinese fishermen caught a giant paddlefish measuring 23 feet (7 meters) and approximately 660 pounds (300 kg) in the Yangtze River.

The paddlefish, also known as the Chinese paddlefish (Psephurus gladius), is critically endangered, and this catch highlighted the need for habitat conservation.

Catching a paddlefish of this size in the Yangtze River involved using specialized fishing techniques to handle large freshwater fish.

The Chinese fishermen employed traditional methods adapted to the unique characteristics of this species.

To capture the giant paddlefish, the fishermen used trawl nets and gillnets, common techniques for catching large fish in rivers.

The nets were large and strong enough to withstand the weight and length of the paddlefish.

The trawl nets were deployed in areas of the Yangtze River where paddlefish are known to frequent.

These fish are often found in the deepest parts of the river, requiring the nets to be strategically placed to intercept their path.

Unlike rod and reel fishing, net fishing does not use bait in the traditional sense. However, the fishermen selected fishing areas based on their knowledge of the paddlefish's migratory and feeding habits.

This fish feeds primarily on plankton and small fish and travels long distances in search of food.

Once the nets were deployed, the fishermen had to wait for the giant paddlefish to swim into them.

When the fish was caught in the net, it began an arduous and coordinated task to bring it to the surface.

The strength and size of the fish made this operation extremely challenging.

The fishermen needed to use all their skills and work as a team to secure the fish and prevent it from escaping or getting injured.

The net was carefully hauled in, and the fishermen used specialized techniques to handle the fish without harming it, given the value and rarity of this species.

Finally, after a prolonged struggle, they managed to pull the paddlefish out of the water and bring it to shore.

The catch was meticulously documented, with measurements and photographs to record the fish's impressive size.

The capture of this giant paddlefish in the Yangtze River in 2007 highlighted the critical situation of this endangered species.

The Chinese paddlefish has suffered a drastic decline in its population due to overfishing, dam construction blocking its migratory routes, and water pollution.

The capture drew the attention of conservationists and scientists, who used the event to emphasize the urgent need to protect the paddlefish's natural habitat and implement more effective conservation measures.

This catch also served to raise public awareness about the fragility of freshwater ecosystems and the importance of the Yangtze River's biodiversity.

15

Alfred Glassell's Black Marlin.

In 1953, Alfred Glassell caught a 1,560-pound (707 kg) black marlin off the coast of Peru.

This catch remains the world record for black marlin and was documented in the film "The Old Man and the Sea," based on the novel by Ernest Hemingway.

Catching a black marlin of this size requires advanced deep-sea fishing techniques, specialized equipment, and great skill on the part of the fisherman.

Alfred Glassell used sport fishing methods adapted to handle the speed and strength of the black marlin, one of the largest and most powerful fish in the ocean.

To capture the giant black marlin, Glassell employed a high-strength fishing rod and a large-capacity reel, specifically designed for catching big fish in deep waters.

The equipment had to withstand long battles and manage the tremendous force and speed of the black marlin.

The fishing line used was extremely strong, probably high-quality monofilament or braid, capable of withstanding the tension exerted by a 1,560-pound fish.

The hook used was large and robust, suitable for securely hooking into the marlin's mouth and resisting its attempts to break free.

The choice of bait was crucial to attract the black marlin.

Glassell used live bait, such as large baitfish (bonitos and mackerels), which are part of the black marlin's natural diet.

These live baits were presented in a way that made them move naturally in the water, simulating the marlin's favorite prey.

The bait was cast in areas of the ocean known to be frequented by marlins, usually near underwater structures like seamounts or reefs, where these large fish hunt.

When the black marlin bit the hook, an epic battle began that lasted several hours.

Black marlins are known for their incredible strength and ability to perform spectacular jumps out of the water, and this specimen was no exception.

The fight was intense, with the marlin making multiple runs and jumps to try to break free.

Glassell had to use all his skill and endurance to manage the rod and reel, maintaining constant pressure to tire the fish without breaking the line.

Catching a black marlin of this size from an offshore boat presented additional challenges, as the sea can be unpredictable and conditions can change.

Finally, after an exhausting battle, Glassell and his team managed to bring the black marlin aboard the boat.

The catch was meticulously documented, with measurements and photographs to record the fish's impressive size.

16

Jakub Vágner's Wels Catfish.

Jakub Vágner, a famous Czech angler, caught an 8.2-foot (2.5-meter) and 220-pound (100 kg) wels catfish in the Po River, Italy, in 2010.

Vágner is known for his extreme expeditions, and this catch was one of his greatest achievements in fishing for large catfish.

Catching a wels catfish of this size requires fishing techniques adapted to handle the strength and endurance of these large freshwater fish.

Jakub Vágner used specialized methods and equipment to maximize his chances of success.

To capture the giant wels catfish, Vágner employed an extremely sturdy fishing rod and a high-capacity reel, designed to withstand the tremendous force of a catfish of this size.

The equipment had to be able to manage long battles and endure constant pressure during the struggle.

The fishing line used was made of very strong material, such as high-quality braid, capable of withstanding extreme tension.

The hook used was large and strong, suitable for securely hooking into the wels catfish's mouth and resisting its powerful attempts to break free.

The choice of bait was crucial to attract the wels catfish, as Vágner used live bait, such as large baitfish (carp and perch), which are part of the natural diet of catfish.

These live baits were presented in a way that made them move naturally in the water, simulating the catfish's favorite prey.

The bait was cast in areas of the Po River known to be frequented by large catfish, typically near submerged structures like logs, rocks, or deep holes where these fish tend to lurk for prey.

When the wels catfish bit the hook, an epic battle began.

Wels catfish are known for their incredible strength and ability to make powerful dives towards the riverbed.

The fight was intense and prolonged, with the catfish making multiple runs and sudden movements to try to break free.

Vágner had to use all his skill and endurance to manage the rod and reel, maintaining constant pressure to tire the fish without breaking the line.

Catching from the shore of the Po River presented additional challenges, as the terrain and river currents made handling the equipment difficult.

Finally, after an exhausting battle, Vágner managed to bring the wels catfish to the shore.

The catch was secured with the help of his team, who worked together to measure and document the impressive size of the catfish before releasing it back into the river.

17

The Giant Carp of Lake Raduta.

In 2013, Colin Smith caught a common carp weighing 101 pounds (46 kg) in Lake Raduta, Romania.

This catch broke the world record for carp and was the result of a long, dedicated, and meticulous fishing session.

Catching a carp of this size requires a combination of skill, patience, and the use of specific fishing techniques adapted for large carp.

Colin Smith employed specialized methods and appropriate equipment to maximize his chances of success.

To capture the giant carp, Smith used a sturdy and flexible fishing rod, specifically designed for catching large carp.

The reel used was high-capacity, capable of handling long stretches of line and providing adequate resistance during the battle with the carp.

The fishing line was made of strong and durable material, probably high-strength monofilament or braid, capable of withstanding the weight and struggle of a 101-pound carp.

The hook used was sharp and high-quality, suitable for securely hooking into the carp's mouth without coming loose during the fight.

The choice of bait was crucial to attract a carp of this size.

Smith used boilies, which are specially formulated dough balls designed to attract carp.

These boilies are made from a mix of flours, proteins, and natural attractants that are irresistible to carp.

Smith also used pre-baiting techniques, which involve throwing large amounts of boilies and other attractive foods into the fishing area for several days before starting to fish.

This creates a feeding area that attracts large carp and keeps them in the zone.

When the carp bit the hook, an intense and prolonged battle began.

Large carp are known for their strength and endurance, and this 101-pound carp was no exception.

The fight involved multiple long and powerful runs, and Smith had to use all his skill and patience to manage the rod and reel.

The battle lasted several hours, during which Smith maintained constant pressure to tire the carp without breaking the line.

Catching from the shore of Lake Raduta presented additional challenges, as the terrain and water conditions could complicate handling the equipment.

Finally, after an exhausting battle, Smith managed to bring the giant carp to shore.

The catch was secured with the help of his team, who worked together to measure and document the impressive size of the carp before releasing it back into the lake.

Colin Smith's capture of this giant carp in 2013 broke the world record and highlighted Smith's skill and dedication as a carp fisherman.

This achievement drew attention to the richness and biodiversity of Lake Raduta, known as a popular destination for big carp fishing.

18

In 2014, Liam O'Connor died in an unusual accident in Alaska while attempting to catch a Chinook salmon.

The fish, known for its size and strength, dragged O'Connor into turbulent waters, where he drowned.

This tragic incident underscores the inherent risks of fishing for large fish in natural environments.

Liam O'Connor, an experienced angler, was participating in a fishing session in one of Alaska's many rivers, known for being home to the Chinook salmon (also called king salmon).

This type of salmon is highly prized by anglers for its impressive size and the fight it offers when being caught.

O'Connor was using high-strength fishing gear designed to withstand the struggle with large salmon.

This included a sturdy rod and a strong reel, with a high-capacity braided fishing line to handle the resistance and runs of the salmon.

To attract the Chinook salmon, O'Connor used specific lures and natural bait, such as salmon eggs and small fish.

These baits are highly effective in attracting salmon due to their natural diet.

While fishing, O'Connor hooked a large Chinook salmon.

The fish, known for its vigor and endurance, began to struggle intensely, making fast and powerful runs.

During the battle, the salmon dragged O'Connor into deeper and more turbulent waters.

As the struggle continued, O'Connor lost his balance and was pulled by the fish into a section of the river with fast currents.

Despite his efforts to maintain control and return to the shore, the powerful currents and the strength of the salmon made it difficult.

Unfortunately, O'Connor was dragged into a part of the river with dangerous rapids, where the currents were too strong.

Although he was an experienced fisherman and a capable swimmer, O'Connor could not free himself from the line or escape the currents and ultimately drowned in the river.

19

Pedro González and the Barracuda in the Caribbean

In 2009, Pedro González, a fisherman in the Caribbean, died in a tragic accident when a barracuda jumped out of the water and bit him on the neck.

Barracudas are known for their sharp teeth and aggressive behavior, making their interactions with humans potentially dangerous.

Pedro González was fishing in Caribbean waters, a region known for its abundant marine life, including large barracudas.

These fish are fast and powerful predators, equipped with sharp teeth that they use to capture their prey.

González was using standard fishing equipment for offshore fishing.

This included a sturdy rod, a strong reel, and a high-strength line, suitable for handling large and aggressive fish like barracudas.

To attract the barracudas, González used bright and artificial lures that mimic small fish.

Lures for barracuda are often brightly colored and designed to move erratically in the water, provoking aggressive attacks from these predators.

While fishing, González hooked a large barracuda.

During the struggle, the fish behaved extremely aggressively, which is typical of this species.

In an unexpected moment, the barracuda leaped out of the water and, in an act of defense or confusion, bit González on the neck.

The barracuda's sharp teeth caused severe injuries, piercing vital arteries and causing severe bleeding.

Despite immediate efforts by other fishermen present to stop the bleeding and provide first aid, the wounds proved to be fatal.

The death of Pedro González in 2009 highlighted the dangers fishermen can face when interacting with large and aggressive marine species.

This accident underscores the need to always be alert and prepared for the unpredictable actions of fish during fishing.

20

John Doe and the Stingray in the Amazon River.

In 2011, a fisherman identified as John Doe died in the Amazon River after being stung by a stingray.

A stingray's sting can be extremely painful and, in rare cases, fatal due to the venom.

John Doe was participating in a fishing session in the Amazon River, a region known for its rich aquatic biodiversity, including various species of stingrays.

Freshwater stingrays in the Amazon are known for their sharp venomous stingers located on their tails, which they use as a defense mechanism.

Doe was using typical river fishing gear, which included a fishing rod, a reel, and a line suitable for catching medium to large-sized fish.

Fishing in the Amazon can be challenging due to the diversity of species and river conditions.

Doe's choice of bait included natural baits such as small fish or invertebrates, which are effective in attracting a variety of species in the Amazon.

However, when fishing in waters inhabited by stingrays, there is an inherent risk of accidental encounters.

While fishing, Doe inadvertently stepped on or disturbed a stingray hidden on the riverbed.

Freshwater stingrays are generally non-aggressive and remain buried in the sediment, but they can quickly attack when they feel threatened.

The stingray, feeling endangered, used its stinger to defend itself, stinging Doe in the leg.

The sting caused a deep and painful wound, injecting venom in the process.

Stingray stings can cause extreme pain, swelling, and, in some cases, severe infections due to the venom and bacteria present in the water.

Doe experienced intense pain and difficulty moving due to the sting.

A stingray sting can cause a toxic reaction that, in rare cases, can be fatal if not treated promptly and properly.

In the isolated environment of the Amazon, the lack of immediate access to medical care worsened the situation.

Despite efforts by other fishermen present to provide first aid and stop the bleeding, Doe succumbed to the complications resulting from the sting.

The conditions in the Amazon, including the difficult access to medical facilities, contributed to the severity of the accident.

21

Michael Stewart and the Shark in South Africa.

In 2018, Michael Stewart was tragically attacked and killed by a great white shark while fishing off the coast of South Africa.

Although Stewart was not attempting to catch the shark, the fish was attracted by the bait and attacked Stewart.

This incident underscores the dangers of fishing in areas inhabited by large marine predators.

Michael Stewart was an experienced fisherman who enjoyed sport fishing in the marine-rich waters of South Africa.

On this occasion, he was participating in an offshore fishing session, a popular activity in the region due to the abundance of various fish species.

Stewart was using standard offshore fishing equipment, which included a sturdy fishing rod, a strong reel, and high-strength lines.

This equipment was suitable for capturing large fish that frequent South African waters.

To attract the large fish Stewart sought to catch, he used large and bloody baits, typical in the fishing of species such as tuna or swordfish.

These baits are effective for attracting target fish, but they can also attract larger predators like great white sharks.

While Stewart was fishing, the bait used began to attract the attention of a large great white shark.

Great white sharks are drawn by the smell of blood and the movements of the bait in the water.

Although Stewart was not attempting to catch the shark, the fish approached the fishing area.

In a tragic and sudden moment, the great white shark attacked Stewart, likely mistaking the movement in the water and the bait for prey.

Great white sharks are known for their strength and speed, and the attack was swift and lethal.

Stewart suffered severe injuries during the attack, and despite the efforts of other fishermen present to help him, the injuries proved to be fatal.

22

Don Henry and the Black Marlin in the Indian Ocean.

In 2010, Don Henry, an Australian fisherman, tragically died while attempting to catch a black marlin in the Indian Ocean.

During the intense struggle, the marlin jumped and injured him with its bill, causing fatal wounds.

This incident underscores the dangers associated with fishing for large predatory fish offshore.

Don Henry was an experienced fisherman known for his passion for deep-sea fishing.

He was participating in a fishing expedition in the Indian Ocean, a region famous for hosting large marlin species, including the black marlin, known for its size, strength, and acrobatic abilities.

Henry was using specialized equipment for offshore fishing, including a high-strength fishing rod, a large and robust reel, and high-capacity fishing lines.

This equipment is essential for handling the tremendous strength and endurance of a black marlin.

To attract the black marlin, Henry used large and bright baits designed to mimic the fish that are part of the marlin's natural diet.

These baits are typically artificial and equipped with large, strong hooks.

During the expedition, Henry hooked a large black marlin.

The fish began to struggle vigorously, making fast runs and acrobatic jumps out of the water, a typical behavior of marlins when hooked.

In one of these jumps, the black marlin launched its body out of the water and, in a sudden twist, injured Henry with its sharp bill.

The impact was violent and direct, causing severe wounds to Henry.

The bills of marlins are extremely sharp and strong, capable of inflicting serious injuries.

The injuries inflicted by the marlin were severe and caused significant bleeding.

Despite the immediate efforts of his team to provide first aid and stop the bleeding, the injuries proved to be fatal.

The speed and force of the marlin's attack left little time for adequate medical attention to be administered.

23

James Haddock and the Sailfish in the Pacific.

In 2013, James Haddock tragically died while fishing in the Pacific.

He caught a sailfish, known for its speed and agility, which jumped and injured him with its sharp bill.

Haddock suffered a severe wound that resulted in fatal bleeding.

James Haddock, an experienced fisherman, was participating in a fishing expedition in the Pacific Ocean, a region famous for its rich waters and the abundance of large game fish, including sailfish.

The sailfish (Istiophorus platypterus) is known for its distinctive dorsal fin and its ability to reach high speeds in the water.

Haddock was using specialized offshore fishing equipment, which included a strong fishing rod, a high-capacity reel, and high-strength fishing lines designed to handle the force and speed of a sailfish.

Additionally, the hooks used were large and robust, suitable for capturing large and fast fish.

To attract the sailfish, Haddock used live baits such as small fish and squid, which are part of the sailfish's natural diet.

These live baits are effective for attracting sailfish due to their natural movement in the water, simulating their prey.

During the expedition, Haddock hooked a large sailfish.

Sailfish are known for their spectacular jumps and fast runs when hooked, and this one was no exception.

During the struggle, the sailfish made several acrobatic jumps out of the water.

In one of these jumps, the sailfish launched its body out of the water and, in a sudden twist, injured Haddock with its sharp bill.

The impact was violent and direct, causing a deep and severe wound.

The bills of sailfish are extremely sharp and can inflict severe wounds due to their speed and strength.

The wound caused by the sailfish's bill resulted in significant bleeding.

Despite the immediate efforts of his team to provide first aid and stop the bleeding, the injuries were too severe.

Haddock suffered fatal hemorrhaging before he could receive adequate medical attention.

24

Henry Wichman and the Swordfish in the Bahamas.

In 2016, Henry Wichman, an experienced fisherman, tragically died while attempting to catch a swordfish in the Bahamas.

The swordfish, known for its speed and strength, mortally wounded Wichman with its sharp bill during the struggle.

This incident underscores the dangers associated with fishing for large predatory fish offshore.

Henry Wichman was a passionate and experienced fisherman, known for his deep-sea fishing skills.

He was participating in a fishing expedition in the crystal-clear waters of the Bahamas, a popular destination for fishing large fish, including swordfish.

Wichman was using specialized offshore fishing equipment, including a sturdy fishing rod, a high-capacity reel, and high-strength fishing lines.

This equipment was suitable for handling the tremendous force and endurance of a swordfish, which can be one of the most challenging fish to catch.

To attract the swordfish, Wichman used live and natural baits, such as squid and small fish, which are part of the swordfish's usual diet.

These baits are effective for attracting swordfish due to their natural movement in the water, simulating their prey.

During the expedition, Wichman hooked a large swordfish.

Swordfish are known for their fast runs and vigorous fight when hooked, and this one was no exception.

During the struggle, the swordfish displayed its impressive strength and speed, making several powerful runs to try to break free.

In a critical moment of the fight, the swordfish jumped out of the water and, in a sudden twist, injured Wichman with its sharp bill.

The impact was violent and direct, causing deep and severe wounds.

The bills of these fish are extremely sharp and can inflict severe injuries due to their speed and strength.

The wound inflicted by the swordfish resulted in significant bleeding.

Despite the immediate efforts of his team to provide first aid and stop the bleeding, the injuries were too severe.

Wichman suffered fatal hemorrhaging before he could receive adequate medical attention.

25

Vampire Fish (Candiru).

In the Amazon River, specimens of candiru, also known as vampire fish, have been captured.

This small fish is known for its habit of parasitizing the gills of larger fish, and there are stories that it can enter the human body.

The candiru (Vandellia cirrhosa) is a small and slender fish that can reach a length of approximately 2.5 cm to 18 cm.

Its body is almost transparent, allowing it to go unnoticed in the water, and it has an elongated, eel-like shape.

The candiru is a parasitic fish known for its unusual feeding method.

This fish enters the gills of larger fish, where it attaches with its spines and feeds on the blood of its host, hence the nickname "vampire fish."

This parasitic behavior is efficient and makes the candiru a highly feared species among the fish in the region.

There are numerous stories about the candiru and its ability to enter the human body, particularly through the urethra.

These stories are generally anecdotal and have not been conclusively confirmed scientifically, however, the fear of the candiru is common among local inhabitants and tourists visiting the Amazon.

Although there are very few documented and verified cases, there are reports of people experiencing pain and injuries supposedly caused by the candiru.

Most of these incidents have been reported by fishermen and swimmers in the Amazon River.

The notoriety of the candiru is largely due to its parasitic behavior and the stories surrounding its interaction with humans.

Although cases of human parasitism are extremely rare and largely unconfirmed, the candiru remains a topic of fascination and fear in the Amazon region.

Precautions:

-Avoid Urinating in the Water: It is recommended to avoid urinating directly in the water while swimming in the Amazon, as this could attract fish seeking warm water currents.

-Personal Protection: Wearing tight-fitting swimwear and adequate protection can help minimize the risk of unwanted encounters with the candiru.

-Local Knowledge: Consulting with local guides and following their advice can help avoid areas where candiru are more common.

Despite its bad reputation, the candiru plays an important role in the Amazon ecosystem.

As a parasite, it helps control the populations of larger fish and contributes to the complex food web of the river.

26

Coelacanth.

In 1938, a South African fisherman caught a coelacanth, a fish thought to have been extinct for 66 million years.

This "living fossil" has lobed fins that resemble the limbs of land-dwelling tetrapods and is an important link in the evolution of vertebrates.

For a long time, the coelacanth was believed to have been extinct since the late Cretaceous period, about 66 million years ago, until its remarkable rediscovery in 1938.

Marjorie Courtenay-Latimer, a museum curator in East London, South Africa, identified the strange fish caught by a local fisherman, which was later confirmed by ichthyologist J.L.B. Smith as a coelacanth.

Coelacanths are often referred to as "living fossils" because they have remained relatively unchanged for hundreds of millions of years.

They belong to a lineage of lobe-finned fishes (Sarcopterygii) that also includes the ancestors of tetrapods, the first vertebrates to walk on land.

The lobed fins of the coelacanth contain bone structures similar to the limbs of tetrapods, providing a crucial evolutionary link between fish and terrestrial vertebrates.

Coelacanths have a distinctive, almost prehistoric appearance.

They can grow up to 2 meters (6.5 feet) in length and weigh up to 90 kilograms (200 pounds).

Their most notable feature is their lobed pectoral and pelvic fins, which are fleshy and limb-like, unlike the ray-finned fins found in most other fishes.

Unique Features:

-Electrosensory Organ: Coelacanths have a rostral organ in their snouts, believed to help them detect electrical signals in their environment, aiding in navigation and hunting in the deep sea.

-Articulated Skull: They possess a unique hinge in their skull, allowing the upper jaw to open wide, which helps in capturing prey.

-Notochord: Instead of a backbone, coelacanths have a notochord, a hollow, pressurized tube that provides support.

Coelacanths are deep-sea fish, typically found at depths between 150 and 700 meters (500 to 2,300 feet).

They inhabit underwater caves and volcanic slopes in the Indian Ocean, near the coasts of East Africa, Indonesia, and Madagascar.

Coelacanths are ovoviviparous, meaning females give birth to live young after the eggs hatch inside their bodies.

This reproductive strategy is rare among fish and adds to the uniqueness of the coelacanth.

Despite their ancient lineage, coelacanths currently face threats from human activities, particularly deep-sea trawling and habitat destruction.

Their slow reproduction rate and specific habitat requirements make them particularly vulnerable to population decline.

Efforts to protect coelacanths include international treaties and the establishment of marine protected areas.

Ongoing scientific research aims to better understand their biology and ecology to inform conservation strategies.

27

Northern Snakehead Fish.

In 2002, a northern snakehead fish was captured in a pond in Crofton, Maryland.

This invasive fish, which can breathe air and move on land, has caused concern due to its potential to disrupt local ecosystems.

The northern snakehead fish (Channa argus) gets its name from its long, cylindrical body and broad, flat head, which resemble those of a snake.

These fish can grow up to 3 feet (about 1 meter) in length and weigh up to 15 pounds (6.8 kg).

They have a mottled brown and tan coloration, which helps them blend into their surroundings.

Unique Features:

-Air-Breathing Capability: Northern snakehead fish have a specialized respiratory system that allows them to breathe atmospheric air. This adaptation enables them to survive in low-oxygen environments and even move short distances on land.

-Terrestrial Mobility: Using a wriggling motion, northern snakehead fish can move on land to find new bodies of water. This ability increases their potential to invade new habitats.

The discovery of the northern snakehead fish in a pond in Crofton, Maryland, in 2002 marked the beginning of widespread concern about this invasive species in the United States.

It is believed that the fish were introduced by aquarium owners who released them into the wild.

After the initial discovery, northern snakehead fish were found in several other states, including Virginia, Delaware, and New York.

Their ability to reproduce quickly and adapt to various environments has facilitated their rapid spread in different bodies of water.

Northern snakehead fish are apex predators in their non-native habitats, feeding on a wide variety of aquatic organisms, including fish, crustaceans, and amphibians.

Their aggressive feeding habits can lead to significant reductions in native species populations.

The introduction of northern snakehead fish into new ecosystems can have cascading effects on the food chain.

By preying on native species and competing with them for resources, northern snakehead fish can disrupt the balance of aquatic ecosystems, potentially leading to a decline in native biodiversity.

The presence of northern snakehead fish can negatively impact local fisheries, as they compete with commercially important fish species.

This competition can lead to reduced catches and economic losses for fishermen and related industries.

The discovery of northern snakehead fish in Maryland prompted a significant response from the public and government.

Efforts to control the population included chemical treatments of affected bodies of water, public education campaigns, and regulations to prevent the transport and release of these fish.

28

Ocean Sunfish (Mola mola).

The ocean sunfish, also known as Mola mola, is one of the largest and heaviest bony fish in the world. It is famous for its round, flattened shape, which makes it look like a large head without a tail.

Mola molas are fascinating and unique creatures that inhabit the world's oceans.

Mola molas can reach a length of over 3 meters (10 feet) and a height of 4.2 meters (14 feet) when measured from fin to fin.

These fish can weigh more than 2,000 kg (4,400 pounds), making them one of the heaviest bony fish in the world.

They have an almost circular body that is extremely flattened laterally.

They lack a traditional tail, and instead, have a structure called a clavus that resembles a truncated fin.

Their dorsal and anal fins are tall and triangular, contributing to their distinctive shape.

The skin of the ocean sunfish is extremely thick and rough, with a texture similar to sandpaper.

It is covered with a mucous layer that can harbor a large number of parasites.

The ocean sunfish is an opportunistic feeder that consumes a variety of marine organisms, though its primary diet consists of jellyfish and other gelatinous zooplankton.

They also eat small fish, zooplankton, squid, and algae and are found in temperate and tropical oceans around the world.

They can swim at great depths but are also frequently seen near the surface, where they are often observed sunbathing.

Mola molas are often seen floating sideways on the water's surface.

This behavior is believed to help regulate their body temperature after diving into colder waters in search of food.

This behavior may also be related to parasite cleaning, as seabirds and small cleaner fish take the opportunity to feed on the parasites on the sunfish's skin.

Mola molas have an extremely high reproductive rate.

Females can release up to 300 million eggs in a spawning season, making them one of the most prolific vertebrates in terms of egg production.

In 2015, a giant sunfish was caught off the coast of Portugal.

This particular specimen stood out for its impressive size, attracting the attention of the scientific community and the general public.

Although they are not listed as endangered, mola molas face several threats, including incidental capture in fishing nets, marine pollution, and climate change.

Aside from human threats, they are also preyed upon by large marine predators such as sharks and orcas.

They can host up to 40 different species of external and internal parasites.

Although little is known about their longevity, they are estimated to live up to 10 years in the wild.

29

Frilled Shark.

In 2007, a living frilled shark was captured by a Japanese fisherman in shallow coastal waters.

This prehistoric shark, which typically lives at depths of up to 1,200 meters, has a long, eel-like body and a mouth full of sharp, curved teeth.

The frilled shark (Chlamydoselachus anguineus), also known as the frill shark, is a rare and fascinating species that has changed little since the age of dinosaurs.

Its name comes from its frilled gills, which have a collar-like appearance around its throat.

This shark has an average length of 1.5 meters, although some can grow up to 2 meters.

Its body is elongated and flexible, giving it an eel-like appearance.

Frilled sharks have a peculiarly wide mouth containing around 300 sharp, curved teeth arranged in 25 rows.

These teeth are designed to trap slippery prey such as squid, fish, and other sharks.

The shape of their teeth and the arrangement of their jaws allow them to firmly grasp their prey and swallow it whole.

This shark prefers deep waters, generally living between 600 and 1,200 meters below the surface, in the abyssal and continental slope zones.

Its capture in shallow waters in 2007 was an unusual event, possibly due to illness or disorientation.

Frilled sharks are ovoviviparous, meaning the embryos develop inside eggs that remain in the mother's body until they are ready to hatch.

They can have between 2 and 15 pups at a time.

The frilled shark is often referred to as a "living fossil" due to its primitive appearance and ancient lineage, which dates back more than 80 million years.

Despite its intimidating appearance, little is known about its behavior and ecology due to the difficulty of studying these animals in their natural deep-water environment.

The capture of a live frilled shark in 2007 attracted the attention of the scientific community and the public, highlighting the hidden biodiversity of the deep sea and the importance of its conservation.

Frilled sharks are not classified as endangered, but their rarity and the increasing pressure from deep-sea trawling pose potential threats to their population.

30

Giant Guitar Fish.

In 2019, fishermen in Thailand caught a rare giant guitar fish, also known as a sharpnose guitarfish.

These fish, which can grow up to 3 meters in length, are a mix between sharks and rays and are critically endangered.

The giant guitarfish (Rhynchobatus djiddensis) is a member of the Rhinobatidae family and is characterized by its flat, elongated body that resembles both sharks and rays.

It has a long, pointed snout and a diamond-shaped body that tapers into a sturdy tail.

This fish has a coloration that varies between shades of gray and brown, with spots and patterns that help it camouflage in the sandy and muddy sea bottoms where it resides.

Giant guitarfish can reach lengths of up to 3 meters and weigh up to 300 kilograms.

They are primarily found in warm and temperate coastal waters from the Indo-Pacific to the Red Sea, although their range has significantly decreased due to overfishing and habitat degradation.

These fish are benthic, meaning they live and feed on the ocean floor.

Their diet includes crustaceans, mollusks, and small fish.

They use their pectoral fins to dig into the sediment in search of food and have flat, robust teeth suitable for crushing shells and hard exoskeletons.

The capture of a giant guitarfish in Thailand in 2019 highlighted the critical situation of this species.

Guitarfish are classified as critically endangered by the International Union for Conservation of Nature (IUCN).

The main threats to their survival are commercial and artisanal fishing, where they are incidentally caught in trawl nets and longlines, as well as habitat loss due to the destruction of coral reefs and mangrove areas.

The conservation of the giant guitarfish is crucial for maintaining the biodiversity of marine ecosystems.

Various conservation efforts are underway to protect this species, including the implementation of marine protected areas, fishing restrictions, and captive breeding programs.

The giant guitarfish is a reminder of the fragility of our marine ecosystems and the need for concerted efforts to protect critically endangered species.

31

Goblin Shark (Mitsukurina owstoni).

In 2014, fishermen off the coast of Florida captured a goblin shark, a rare species that lives at depths of up to 1,300 meters.

This shark is distinguished by its long "nose" and its jaw that projects forward to capture prey.

The goblin shark (Mitsukurina owstoni) is one of the most enigmatic and bizarre creatures of the ocean.

It is known for its prehistoric appearance, with a body that can reach lengths of between 3 and 4 meters.

Its most distinctive feature is its elongated, flattened snout, also known as a "rostrum," which is equipped with special sensory organs that detect the electric fields produced by its prey.

The goblin shark's jaw is another fascinating aspect.

This shark has highly protrusible jaws that can quickly extend forward to catch its prey, which includes fish, squid, and crustaceans.

Its teeth are long, thin, and pointed, suitable for grabbing slippery prey in the deep ocean.

The goblin shark inhabits the deep waters of the Atlantic, Pacific, and Indian Oceans, typically at depths between 200 and 1,300 meters.

Because it lives at such depths, it is rarely seen by humans and very little is known about its behavior and biology.

The capture of a goblin shark in shallower waters near Florida in 2014 was an unusual event and attracted considerable scientific and media attention.

Goblin sharks are pink in color due to the blood vessels visible through their translucent skin.

This color can vary depending on the depth at which they live, with deeper individuals tending to be darker in color.

The skin of the goblin shark is smooth and lacks the typical tough scales of other sharks, giving it a unique appearance.

Despite their intimidating appearance, goblin sharks do not pose a threat to humans due to the great depths they inhabit and their rare interaction with people.

They are considered a "living fossil" because their lineage dates back about 125 million years, remaining virtually unchanged since prehistoric times.

The capture of a goblin shark provides a valuable opportunity for scientists to study this rare and little-known species.

Research can provide crucial information about their ecology, reproduction, and role in deep-sea ecosystems.

However, it also underscores the importance of conserving deep-sea habitats, which are threatened by human activities such as trawling and oil and gas exploration.

32

Deep-Sea Dragonfish (Bathysaurus ferox).

In 2017, a deep-sea dragonfish (Bathysaurus ferox) was captured in the depths of the Atlantic Ocean.

This abyssal fish has a terrifying and bioluminescent appearance and lives at depths of up to 2,000 meters, where it uses its bioluminescence to attract prey.

The deep-sea dragonfish is a formidable predator in deep-sea ecosystems.

Its elongated and slender body, which can reach lengths of up to 60 cm, is perfectly adapted to life in the dark depths of the ocean.

Its generally dark coloration helps it blend into the low-light environment where it resides.

One of the most notable features of the deep-sea dragonfish is its bioluminescent capability.

It possesses light-producing organs called photophores located along its body and particularly around its jaw.

This bioluminescence is used to attract prey, which is essential in an environment where sunlight does not penetrate.

Deep-sea dragonfish produce light through chemical reactions in these photophores, creating flashes that can attract curious fish and crustaceans toward their deadly jaws.

The mouth of the deep-sea dragonfish is large and filled with sharp, transparent teeth perfect for capturing and holding onto prey.

These teeth can even retract backward to ensure that captured prey cannot escape.

Its lower jaw is equipped with a luminous appendage that acts as a lure, moving in the darkness to attract prey closer to its jaws.

The eyes of the deep-sea dragonfish are adapted for low-light vision, allowing them to detect movements and light signals in their environment.

These visual adaptations are crucial for their survival in the bathypelagic zone, an extremely dark and high-pressure place.

The habitat of the deep-sea dragonfish is found on the continental slopes and underwater canyons of the Atlantic Ocean.

Living at depths of up to 2,000 meters means these creatures are adapted to extreme pressures and very low temperatures.

Their metabolism is slow, allowing them to survive with the scarce food opportunities at these depths.

The capture of a deep-sea dragonfish in 2017 provided scientists with a unique opportunity to study this mysterious creature.

Each capture from these depths offers valuable insights into the biology, behavior, and adaptation of abyssal organisms.

Through these studies, researchers can learn more about deep-sea ecosystems and how creatures like the deep-sea dragonfish play a role in these complex food webs.

33

Stonefish (Synanceia).

In 2011, a fisherman in Australia captured a stonefish
(Synanceia), known as one of the most venomous fish
in the world.

This fish has dorsal spines that inject an extremely painful
and potentially fatal venom.

The stonefish is famous for its near-perfect camouflage,
allowing it to blend in with its rocky or coral reef environment,
making it virtually invisible to both its prey and humans.

This camouflage protects it from predators and allows it to
ambush its prey with ease.

Its body is robust and covered with growths and
protuberances that resemble algae and rocks.

One of the most dangerous features of the stonefish is its
dorsal spines, which are connected to venom glands.

When it feels threatened or is accidentally stepped on,
the stonefish erects these spines and can inject its potent
venom.

The venom of this fish contains neurotoxins that can cause
extreme pain, swelling, tissue necrosis, paralysis, and even
death if not treated promptly.

The sting is so painful that it has been described as one of
the most agonizing experiences a human can endure.

The treatment for a stonefish sting generally includes immersing the affected area in hot water, as hot as the victim can tolerate, since heat can help break down the toxins in the venom.

However, immediate medical attention is crucial, and in many cases, the administration of antivenom and treatment for severe pain are needed.

The habitat of the stonefish includes the coastal waters of the Indo-Pacific, particularly in coral reef regions and sandy and rocky bottoms.

It prefers shallow areas, which increases the likelihood of encounters with swimmers and divers.

Despite its dangerous venom, the stonefish plays an important role in its ecosystem as a predator.

It feeds on small fish and crustaceans, which it captures through a quick ambush using its excellent camouflage to get close to its prey before sucking them into its mouth with impressive speed.

The capture of a stonefish in Australia in 2011 underscored the need for caution and respect when interacting with marine habitats.

Accidental encounters with stonefish can be avoided by wearing protective footwear and paying attention to the seabed areas where these fish might be camouflaged.

In terms of conservation, although the stonefish is not currently endangered, the health of its populations is linked to the preservation of coral reefs and the marine ecosystems it inhabits.

34

Tides.

Tides play a crucial role in fishing, affecting both commercial and recreational fishermen.

Understanding how tides influence fishing activity can significantly increase the chances of success.

Types of Tides:

-High Tides (High Water): Water covers areas that are usually exposed, allowing fish to access new habitats and food sources. Fish often venture into marsh areas, estuaries, and coastal zones in search of prey. Fishermen usually find more fish near the shore during high tide.

-Low Tides (Low Water): During these times, water recedes, exposing sandbanks, rocks, and other intertidal habitats. This can concentrate fish in channels and tide pools, making them more accessible to fishermen.
However, some species may move to deeper waters to avoid being stranded.

-Spring Tides: These occur during the new moon and full moon, when the gravity of the sun and moon combine to produce more extreme tides. These tides have a greater tidal range (difference between high and low tide), which can increase fish activity due to rapid changes in water level and strong currents.

-Neap Tides: These happen during the first and third quarters of the moon, when the sun and moon are at right angles to the Earth, producing tides with a smaller range. Currents are weaker during neap tides, which can make fish less active.

35

Tidal Currents.

Tidal currents can influence fish behavior, food distribution, and the location of productive fishing spots.

-Flood Currents: These occur when the tide is rising and water moves towards the shore. Flood currents fill estuaries, bays, and marshes. Fish often follow flood currents into flooded areas in search of food. Flood currents can carry nutrients and small organisms, attracting predatory fish. This is a good time to fish near coastal structures and estuary entrances.

-Ebb Currents: These occur when the tide is falling and water moves from the shore to the open sea. Fish may follow ebb currents towards the open sea. Ebb currents can concentrate fish in channels and tide pools. This is a good time to fish in channels and river mouths, where fish concentrate as they leave the estuary.

-Spring Tides: These occur during the new moon and full moon, when the gravitational forces of the sun and moon combine to produce more extreme tides. Tidal currents are stronger and can move large amounts of water and nutrients. Spring tides can increase fish activity due to rapid changes in water level. They can provide excellent fishing opportunities near underwater structures and areas with strong currents.

-Neap Tides: These occur during the first and last quarters of the moon, when the gravitational forces of the sun and moon are at right angles, producing tides with a smaller range. Tidal currents are weaker and less pronounced. Fish activity may be lower due to the more gradual changes in water level. These can be more challenging times for fishing in areas that rely on strong currents for fish concentration.

-Influx and Displacement Currents: These are horizontal movements of water to and from the coast, not necessarily tied to tides. Influx currents can bring nutrients and attract fish towards the shore. Displacement currents can carry fish to deeper waters. Fishermen should pay attention to these currents to identify productive areas at different times of the day.

-Slack Tide Currents: These occur during the brief period when the tide changes from flood to ebb or vice versa, and the movement of the water is minimal. It can be a good time to fish for species that prefer calm waters. Catches may temporarily decrease due to the lack of water movement that distributes nutrients and prey. This is a time to change strategy or location in response to changing conditions.

-Eddies: These are circular currents that form when the main tidal currents encounter obstacles such as islands, rocks, or underwater structures. They can concentrate fish and nutrients in specific areas. Eddies can create turbulence zones that are attractive to predatory fish. It is important to identify these patterns to take advantage of fishing opportunities at these spots.

36

Moon Phases.

The phase of the moon has a significant impact on fishing due to its influence on tides and fish behavior.

-New Moon: In this phase, the moon is positioned between the Earth and the Sun, so its illuminated side is not visible from Earth. The new moon produces spring tides, with greater differences between high and low tides. These strong currents can mobilize large amounts of nutrients, attracting fish. Many fishermen find that fish are more active and aggressive in their feeding during the new moon. The darkness of the night can also make fish less cautious. The lack of light can make night fishing more productive for certain species that feed more actively in the dark.

-Waxing Crescent: This is the phase after the new moon, when the illuminated portion of the moon increases each night. The tides during the waxing crescent are less extreme than spring tides but can still provide good tidal activity. As the moon becomes more visible, fish activity may also increase. Fish may begin to feed more as the moonlight grows. The early and late hours of light can be especially productive, as fish feed actively during these times.

-First Quarter: In this phase, the right half of the moon is illuminated and visible from Earth. The tides are weaker and less extreme compared to spring tides. The gentler currents can be beneficial for certain species that prefer more stable conditions. Fish activity can be more predictable, making it a good time to fish in less turbulent waters.

-Full Moon: This occurs when the moon is fully illuminated and visible from Earth. Similar to the new moon, the full moon produces spring tides with strong currents. The full moon provides additional light during the night, which can increase the activity of nocturnal fish. Many fish species feed more actively during the full moon. Night fishing can be especially productive due to the increased visibility and fish activity.

-Waning Gibbous: This is the phase after the full moon, when the illuminated portion of the moon decreases each night. Tides begin to decrease in intensity but can still provide good tidal activity. As the moon wanes, fish activity may decrease. However, there are still good opportunities for fishing. Similar to the waxing crescent phase, fish may be more active during the early and late hours of daylight.

-Last Quarter: In this phase, the left half of the moon is illuminated and visible from Earth. Tides are weaker and less extreme, which can be beneficial for fishing in less turbulent waters. Fish activity can be more predictable, similar to the first quarter phase.

-Balsamic Phase (Dark Moon): This phase occurs just before the new moon, when the moon is barely visible and almost completely dark. Tides are very mild, with little difference between high and low tide. Fish activity may be low due to the lack of light and minimal currents. It can be more productive to fish during the day in this phase, as nocturnal activity is low.

37

For over 4,000 years, humanity has used fishing rods, dating back to around 2000 B.C.

These tools have been found in various cultures, including Egypt, China, Greece, and Trinidad and Tobago.

Initially, fishing rods were simple branches used to better manipulate the line tied to a hook.

These early fishing rods were rudimentary but effective for their purpose.

The earliest recorded hook dates back approximately 4,200 years and was discovered on the island of Timor in Southeast Asia.

This ancient hook was made of bone, reflecting the creativity and technical skills of ancient civilizations in making fishing tools.

The presence of these primitive hooks suggests that fishing was an important activity for ancient communities, both as a source of food and for other purposes such as trade and survival.

38

The largest hook in the world is located in the state of Florida, USA.

It has an impressive length of 3.20 meters and weighs over 161 kilograms.

This giant hook is a testament to the creativity and skills of fishermen and stands out as a unique attraction in Florida's fishing community.

Although its practical use may be limited due to its massive size, it is undoubtedly an impressive piece that draws the attention of fishing enthusiasts and tourists alike.

On the other hand, the smallest fishing rod in the world is a marvel of miniaturization.

At only 20 centimeters in length, this tiny fishing rod is almost as small as a standard ruler and can extend to approximately one meter in total length.

Despite its diminutive size, this fishing rod is functional and can be used to catch small fish in situations where ultralight equipment is required.

With an affordable price of around 13 euros, this mini fishing rod is a fun and economical option for fishing enthusiasts looking for something out of the ordinary.

39

The most expensive lure on the planet is a true masterpiece of ostentation and exclusivity.

Made by the company Mac Daddy, this lure has an incredible price of 1 million dollars.

With an impressive length of 30 centimeters, it is made from luxurious materials, including 1.4 kilograms of gold and platinum.

But what really makes it stand out are the adornments: it is decorated with 100 carats of diamonds and rubies, making it a unique piece of jewelry.

Beyond its function as a fishing lure, this object is a symbol of opulence and extravagance.

On the other hand, the most expensive fishing rod in the world is an example of Japanese craftsmanship and exceptional quality.

Priced at 8,000 euros, this fishing rod offers top-level performance:

-It has a length of 5.7 meters and consists of 4 sections. When closed, it measures 172 centimeters and weighs 1.6 kilograms.

-With a maximum diameter at the top of 24.4 millimeters and a bottom end diameter of 15 millimeters, this rod is designed to handle heavy loads.

-It can support a maximum weight of 130 grams and is rated for lines up to 100 pounds (PE 15).

40

Ernest Hemingway is undoubtedly one of the most famous fishermen of all time, and his passion for fishing is reflected both in his personal achievements and his literary work.

Hemingway was known for his skill in marlin fishing, and his record of having caught seven marlins in a single day is legendary in the world of sport fishing.

However, beyond his feats as a fisherman, he is primarily recognized for his masterpiece "The Old Man and the Sea."

Published in 1952, this novel is a poignant tale about an old Cuban fisherman, Santiago, and his epic struggle to catch a great swordfish in the sea.

Through this story, Hemingway captures the very essence of the human struggle against nature, perseverance in the face of adversity, and dignity in defeat.

"The Old Man and the Sea" not only solidified Hemingway's reputation as one of the great writers of the 20th century but also elevated his status as an iconic figure in the fishing world.

His passion for fishing and his ability to capture the human experience in the context of life at sea make him a legendary figure who continues to inspire both fishermen and writers alike.

41

Fishing Rod Guides.

Also known as guides or eyes, they play a fundamental role in modern rod fishing by providing a guiding system for the fishing line along the rod.

This innovation was a significant development in the evolution of fishing rods and had a notable impact on the technique and effectiveness of sport fishing.

The history of fishing rod guides dates back to the 18th century, where the English fisherman and writer Izaak Walton (also known as Isaac Walton) is credited with being one of the pioneers in their use.

Walton is known for his influential work "The Compleat Angler," published in 1653, which is considered one of the most important treatises on fishing in English literature.

Although the use of guides is not specifically mentioned in this work, Walton significantly contributed to the promotion and dissemination of fishing as a recreational activity.

The incorporation of guides into fishing rods allowed the line to move more smoothly and reduced friction, improving casting accuracy and fishing efficiency.

Over time, guides have been developed and refined, using a variety of materials such as ceramic, stainless steel, and titanium to provide optimal guidance for the fishing line.

42

Superstitions.

-Evil Eye: Some fishermen believe that certain people can negatively influence their fishing simply by looking at them, a belief known as the "evil eye." To avoid this, they may perform rituals or carry protective amulets.

-Greeting the Sea: Before going out to fish, it is common for fishermen to perform a gesture of greeting to the sea, such as throwing a coin into the water or reciting a prayer, as a way to obtain the ocean's blessing and protection.

-Clothing Colors: Some fishermen believe that certain colors of clothing can attract or repel fish. For example, yellow is considered bad luck in some cultures, while white or blue is seen as more auspicious.

-No Singing on the Boat: There is a superstition that singing or whistling on a boat can attract storms or scare away fish. Therefore, some fishermen avoid making unnecessary noise while at sea.

-Small Rituals Before Fishing: Before casting the hook, some fishermen perform small rituals, such as tapping the fishing rod three times on the ground or tying a special knot in the line, as a way to attract good luck.

-Not Mentioning the Word "Fish" on Land: Some people believe that mentioning the word "fish" while on land can scare away the fish and make fishing more difficult. Therefore, they prefer to use euphemisms or avoid talking about fishing until they are on the water.

-Touching the Fish's Tail: After catching a fish, some fishermen gently touch the fish's tail as a gesture of thanks, ensuring good luck for future catches.

-No Bananas on the Boat: Many fishermen believe that bringing bananas on board a boat brings bad luck. This superstition dates back to the days when fruit would quickly rot and attract insects, which could ruin the fishing trip.

-No Throwing Trash into the Sea: There is a belief that throwing trash into the sea can anger the "water spirits" and bring bad omens for fishing. Therefore, fishermen tend to be environmentally respectful and avoid dumping waste into the ocean.

-Watch Out for Seagulls: Some fishermen believe that if seagulls are flying low or near the boat, it is a sign of good fishing. However, if the seagulls fly very high or quickly move away, it can be a bad omen.

-No Fishing in Murky or Turbulent Waters: Many fishermen believe that fishing in turbulent or dirty waters is not only less productive but can also bring bad luck or danger. They prefer to wait for the waters to be calmer and clearer.

-Talking to the Fish: Some fishermen believe that talking to the fish can increase their chances of catching them. Whether to encourage the fish to bite the hook or simply as a way to pass the time, this practice is common in some fishing cultures.

-Placing the Hook Upside Down: Some fishermen believe that placing the hook upside down, with the point towards the handle, can attract larger fish or increase the chances of a big catch. This practice may vary according to region and local tradition.

-Throwing a Coin into the Sea: Before setting out on a fishing trip, some fishermen throw a coin into the sea as an offering to the water gods or as a gesture of good luck. This is related to the idea of earning the favor of the elements before venturing into unknown waters.

43

Top Fish Producers Worldwide.

The top ten fish producers worldwide, along with their respective annual productions in tons, are as follows:

-China: 72.8 million tons (including 13.1 million tons from capture and the rest from aquaculture). China is the world's largest fish producer, leading in both capture fisheries and aquaculture. Its vast aquaculture network and extensive coastlines contribute significantly to its high production.

-Indonesia: 21.8 million tons. Indonesia, with its numerous archipelagos and biodiversity-rich waters, is a leader in capture fisheries, especially for tuna and shrimp, and has developed a robust aquaculture industry.

-India: 14.4 million tons. India has seen significant growth in its fish production, especially in aquaculture, with the farming of species like rohu and catfish, as well as in capture fisheries along its vast coastlines and rivers.

-Vietnam: 8.2 million tons. Vietnam is known for its aquaculture production, particularly in farming pangasius and shrimp, which are exported worldwide.

-Peru: 6.7 million tons. Peru is a giant in capture fisheries, especially for anchoveta, which is primarily used for fishmeal and fish oil production.

-United States: 5.2 million tons. The United States has a diverse fishing industry, including both capture fisheries for species like salmon and tuna, and aquaculture for oysters and catfish.

-Japan: 4.1 million tons. Japan, with its rich fishing tradition, excels in the capture of species such as tuna, salmon, and various saltwater fish species.

-Russia: 4.5 million tons. Russia, with vast coastlines in the Arctic and Pacific Oceans, is a major fish producer, especially for species like cod and salmon.

-Norway: 4.2 million tons. Norway is a world leader in salmon aquaculture and also has a strong capture fishing industry, particularly for cod and herring.

-Chile: 3.7 million tons. Chile is known for its salmon aquaculture production, being one of the world's largest exporters, and also has a significant capture fishing industry.

44

The Humboldt Current.

Also known as the Peruvian Current, it is one of the most important ocean currents in the world.

It originates in the cold waters of southern Chile and moves northward along the western coast of South America up to Ecuador.

The Humboldt Current is a cold, nutrient-rich current due to the upwelling of deep waters.

This upwelling brings essential nutrients to the surface, fostering high biological productivity.

Approximately 20% of the world's fish production comes from the Humboldt Current.

This high productivity is the basis of a rich marine biodiversity and a thriving fishing industry, especially in Peru and Chile.

Among the most important species are the Peruvian anchoveta, jack mackerel, mackerel, and sardines.

These species are fundamental to the economy of coastal countries and are also a crucial food source for other marine species.

The Humboldt Current has a moderating effect on the coastal climate of Chile, Peru, and Ecuador, keeping coastal temperatures cooler and contributing to the aridity of the Atacama Desert.

The Humboldt Current is vital for both marine ecology and local economies.

The high productivity of the current supports one of the largest fisheries in the world.

Peru, for example, is one of the leading producers of fishmeal and fish oil, thanks to the abundant catches of anchoveta.

Despite its importance, the Humboldt Current and the species that depend on it face significant threats, such as overfishing and climate change.

El Niño events can significantly warm the waters and reduce upwelling, negatively impacting fish populations.

It is crucial to implement sustainable fishing practices and conservation measures to protect this vital ecosystem.

45

**In prehistoric times, people tried
to catch fish with their bare hands.**

This technique is known as hand fishing.

However, as they developed more skills and tools, they began
to use more effective methods to catch fish.

Primitive tools included harpoons and spears, made of wood and
stone, which allowed fishermen to reach and catch fish from the
shore or in shallow waters.

Nets were another significant advancement in fishing technology.

Initially made from plant fibers and later from animal tendons and
skins, nets allowed the capture of multiple fish at once.

These nets could be cast, submerged, or spread in the water to
catch swimming fish.

In addition to harpoons, spears, and nets, various types of traps
were used.

Stone traps and funnel traps were common; the latter consisted of
conical structures that guided fish into an enclosed area from which
they could not escape.

Cage traps, made of branches and other natural materials, were
placed in streams and estuaries to capture fish swimming with the
current.

The evolution of these techniques demonstrates human capacity to
innovate and adapt to their environment, ensuring a constant food
source and contributing to the development of human societies.

The combination of manual skills and sophisticated tools allowed
prehistoric fishermen to capture a greater quantity and variety of
fish, which in turn supported the growth of communities.

46

The fastest fish in the ocean is the marlin, known for its ability to swim at impressive speeds of up to 129 km/h (80 mph).

This speed is facilitated by its hydrodynamic body and dorsal fin, which reduces water resistance.

Marlins are efficient predators and use their speed to hunt prey such as fish and cephalopods.

There are several species of marlin, including the blue marlin, black marlin, striped marlin, and white marlin, all of which are valued in both sport fishing and the fishing industry.

The streamlined design of the marlin's body reduces water resistance, allowing it to move at high speeds.

The marlin's dorsal fin can fold into a groove in its body to minimize friction during fast swimming.

The marlin's strong and well-developed muscles provide the necessary power for its rapid accelerations.

A lightweight yet strong skeleton contributes to its ability to swim quickly without adding unnecessary weight.

Marlins use their speed to hunt fish and cephalopods, often attacking their prey from below or behind.

47

The fishing technique known as "fly fishing" originated in ancient Rome.

This method was first described by the Roman writer Claudius Aelianus in the 2nd century AD in his work "De Natura Animalium."

Aelianus described how fishermen in Macedonia used an artificial lure, a fly made of wool and feathers, to attract and capture fish in the Asterius River.

Fly fishing imitates aquatic insects and other organisms that are food for fish, using a light line and a flexible rod to cast the lure accurately.

Over time, fly fishing evolved and became popular in Europe and North America, becoming a sophisticated technique appreciated for both its effectiveness and the skill and art it requires.

Fly fishing is especially effective for catching trout, salmon, and other freshwater fish, although it is also used in marine environments for species such as bass and swordfish.

48

The Salmon.

The salmon is an anadromous fish, meaning it is born in freshwater, migrates to the ocean to live most of its life, and then returns to rivers to spawn.

One of the most impressive characteristics of salmon is their ability to swim long distances upstream, up to 1,500 km, to reach their birthplace.

This migration is driven by a strong instinct to reproduce and is crucial for the survival of the species.

During this journey, salmon face numerous challenges, such as rapids, dams, and predators.

They use their sense of smell to identify the specific river where they were born, allowing them to return precisely to their spawning grounds.

The salmon migration is a vital ecological phenomenon, contributing to the health of river ecosystems by providing nutrients and forming a crucial part of the food chain.

49

Some fish have the ability to change sex during their lifetime, a phenomenon known as sequential hermaphroditism.

In this process, a fish can change from female to male (protogyny) or from male to female (protandry) depending on factors such as age, size, and the social structure of its population.

Examples of fish that exhibit sequential hermaphroditism include some species of grouper, wrasses, and damselfish.

Additionally, some species of fish can produce sounds to communicate with each other.

They use different methods to generate these sounds, such as using muscles associated with their swim bladder, rubbing their fins, teeth, or bones together.

This acoustic communication ability can be used for various functions, including mate attraction, territory defense, and the coordination of movements in schools.

Examples of fish that produce sounds include the drum fish and the toadfish.

50

Bioluminescence is the ability of some organisms to produce their own light through chemical reactions.

This phenomenon is common in the deep ocean, where sunlight does not penetrate.

Bioluminescent fish use this ability for various functions, such as communication, attracting prey, camouflage, and defense against predators.

Among bioluminescent fish are the lanternfish (Myctophidae), which uses its bioluminescence to attract prey and communicate with each other; the dragonfish (Stomiidae), which emits light to attract prey and possibly to camouflage itself; and the hatchetfish (Sternoptychidae), whose bioluminescence helps it to camouflage in the dim light of the deep ocean.

Some species of fish have the ability to generate electric discharges.

This ability can serve for defense, hunting prey, and communication.

Among electric fish are the electric eel (Electrophorus electricus), which generates strong electric discharges to stun its prey and defend itself from predators; the electric catfish (Malapterurus electricus), which uses electric discharges to hunt and defend itself; and the elephantfish (Mormyridae), which emits weak electric pulses for navigation and communication in murky waters.

51

The fishing technique called "gillnetting" uses nets designed to catch fish by their mouth or gills.

These nets consist of mesh panels that are placed vertically in the water, allowing fish to try to swim through them.

However, due to the mesh size, fish become trapped when they try to back out, as their gills or mouth get entangled in the net.

This method is highly effective and is used in various areas of the world to catch a wide variety of fish species.

Gillnets are made of nylon or other durable synthetic materials.

The mesh size determines what type of fish will be caught, allowing for selective fishing.

Gillnets can be fixed, anchored to the seabed, or drifting, floating freely and carried by currents.

Fish swim toward the net, and their heads pass through the mesh; when they try to back out, they get caught by the gills or mouth, preventing them from escaping.

The advantages of this technique include its selectivity, as it allows for the selection of fish size by adjusting the mesh size, and its efficiency, as it can capture large quantities of fish in a single deployment.

However, it also has disadvantages, such as the incidental catch of unwanted or juvenile species, which can negatively impact marine ecosystems, and environmental impact, as improper management can cause damage to marine habitats and contribute to overfishing.

52

Some species of fish have the ability to jump out of the water to catch insects that are on the surface.

A notable example of this ability is the archerfish (Toxotes jaculatrix), known for its unique hunting technique.

The archerfish uses its mouth to shoot jets of water at insects perched on nearby vegetation, knocking them into the water where they can be easily captured.

In addition to the archerfish, other species like salmon and trout can also jump out of the water, though they generally do this to overcome obstacles during their migrations rather than to hunt insects.

However, the archerfish is the most specialized in this technique, showing remarkable precision and strength in its water jets, which can reach distances of up to one meter.

53

The fishing technique called "purse seining" uses a large circular net designed to surround and capture fish in one place.

This method is highly effective for capturing large quantities of pelagic fish, such as tuna, mackerel, and herring.

The purse seine net is deployed from a vessel and then closed at the bottom using a cable or rope, forming a pouch that traps the fish.

This process prevents the fish from escaping by swimming downward.

Once the net is closed, its size is gradually reduced to concentrate the fish and facilitate their collection.

Purse seining is an efficient and widely used technique in commercial fishing due to its ability to capture large volumes of fish in a single haul.

However, it must be carefully managed to avoid the incidental catch of unwanted species and minimize environmental impact.

54

Some fish, such as the flying fish, have modified fins that allow them to leap out of the water and glide through the air.

These elongated and strong pectoral fins act like wings, enabling the flying fish (family Exocoetidae) to glide over the water's surface for up to 200 meters to escape predators.

Another example is the hatchetfish (family Sternoptychidae), which uses its pectoral fins and adapted musculature to make quick, short jumps out of the water, helping them evade predators.

Additionally, the archerfish (family Toxotidae) can jump to capture prey in nearby vegetation, although its primary technique is shooting jets of water to knock down insects.

Another notable fish is the needlefish, which can jump and skim over the water's surface to avoid being caught.

These adaptations demonstrate the diversity of strategies that fish have developed to survive and thrive in their aquatic environments, using jumping and gliding both to escape predators and to capture prey.

55

**The total number of commercial fishers
and aquaculturists is estimated
at 38 million worldwide.**

Fishing and aquaculture provide direct and indirect
employment to more than 500 million people,
highlighting their global economic importance.

In addition to being a crucial source of food, modern
fishing is also a popular recreational pastime.

In the United States, over 44 million people enjoy
fishing each year, and an average angler spends
approximately $1,261 annually on this activity.

One million Americans spend an average of 17 days
fishing each year.

In Canada, around 3.2 million people participate in
recreational fishing, spending an average of CAD
$2,150 annually.

In Australia, approximately 3.4 million people enjoy
recreational fishing, spending an average of AUD
$1,600 per year.

Fishing not only contributes significantly to the global
economy but also provides enjoyment and relaxation
for millions of people around the world.

56

The best freshwater fishing spots in the world.

-The Pantanal, Brazil: Located in the Central-West region of Brazil, the Pantanal is famous for sport fishing in freshwater. It is home to species such as peacock bass, pacu, pintado, and dorado.

-Lake Victoria, Africa: The largest lake in Africa, spanning Uganda, Kenya, and Tanzania, is renowned for Nile perch and tilapia fishing.

-Lake Baikal, Russia: The deepest lake in the world, situated in Siberia, is known for its variety of endemic species, such as omul and Baikal sturgeon.

-Mekong River, Southeast Asia: This river flows through several countries, including Thailand and Cambodia, and is known for giant catfish and Siamese carp fishing.

-Lake Bled, Slovenia: Famous for its scenic beauty, this alpine lake offers fishing for brown trout, rainbow trout, and carp.

-Lake Taupo, New Zealand: The largest volcanic lake in New Zealand is known for its rainbow trout and brown trout fishing.

-Great Lakes, North America: These lakes, including Lake Superior, Michigan, Huron, Erie, and Ontario, are famous for salmon, trout, and perch fishing.

-Lake Malawi, Africa: This lake, located between Malawi, Mozambique, and Tanzania, is home to a great diversity of cichlids, popular among sport fishers.

-Amazon River, South America: The largest river in the world, flowing through several South American countries, is known for fishing exotic species such as arapaima, piranha, and payara.

-Lake St. Clair, USA and Canada: Located between Ontario and Michigan, this lake is popular for northern pike, muskie, and yellow perch fishing.

57

The best places in the world for saltwater sport fishing.

-Great Barrier Reef, Australia: Famous for its marine biodiversity, offering fishing for marlin, tuna, and sailfish in its crystal-clear waters.

-Kona Coast, Hawaii: Known for its deep waters close to shore, Kona is an excellent spot for fishing blue and black marlin, as well as tuna and mahi-mahi.

-Cabo San Lucas, Mexico: Located at the tip of the Baja California Peninsula, Cabo San Lucas is popular for marlin, sailfish, and mahi-mahi fishing.

-Maldives: Offers a world-class fishing experience, with abundant catches of tuna, wahoo, sailfish, and marlin.

-Florida Coast, USA: Especially the Florida Keys, is famous for fishing sailfish, marlin, tuna, mahi-mahi, and wahoo.

-Seychelles: These Indian Ocean islands are known for marlin, sailfish, tuna, and wahoo fishing in a paradise-like setting.

-Costa Rica: The Pacific coast of Costa Rica is a world-renowned sport fishing destination, famous for its abundance of sailfish, marlin, mahi-mahi, and tuna.

-Mauritius: The waters of Mauritius are rich in marlin, tuna, and sailfish, attracting anglers from around the world.

-Cairns, Australia: Another hot spot in Australia for black and blue marlin fishing, as well as tuna and wahoo.

-Bermuda: Offers excellent blue marlin, tuna, and wahoo fishing, with sport fishing tournaments that attract anglers from everywhere.

58

Cormorant Fishing Technique.

The technique of cormorant fishing has been practiced for centuries in China and Japan, with historical records dating back over 1,300 years.

In China, this practice has been documented since the Tang Dynasty (618-907 AD), while in Japan, it has been used since the Nara period (710-794 AD).

Cormorants, expert aquatic birds in fish capture, are trained from a young age to assist in fishing.

The training process includes:

-Imprinting: Cormorant chicks are hand-raised to become accustomed to humans.

-Gradual Training: They are taught to catch fish and return them without ingesting, often starting with small fish.

-Use of Rings: Rings are placed at the base of the cormorant's neck to prevent them from swallowing large fish, allowing them to only swallow small fish as a reward.

During fishing, the fishermen navigate in boats and carry several trained cormorants.

The birds are released into the water and dive to catch fish.

Once a fish is caught, the cormorant returns to the boat, and the fisherman retrieves the fish from the bird's beak.

This technique is effective for capturing species such as carp and trout.

In some regions, demonstrations are held for tourists, showcasing the skill and tradition of this ancient practice.

59

Ice Fishing.

Ice fishing is a popular activity in cold regions where fishermen drill holes in the ice of frozen lakes and rivers to access the water and fish.

This technique is mainly practiced in countries such as Canada, the United States, Russia, and the Nordic countries.

Methods of Ice Fishing:

-Rod Fishing: Using short fishing rods specifically designed for ice fishing.
-Hand Line Fishing: Using a fishing line without a rod, which is lowered directly into the water.
-Tip-ups: Devices placed over the hole that detect when a fish bites the hook, raising a flag as a signal.

Most Common Fish:

-Trout: Species such as rainbow trout and lake trout.
-Pike: Known for its size and aggressiveness.
-Perch: Common in many lakes.
-Walleye: Highly sought after for its flavor.
-Crappie: Popular for its abundance and ease of catch.

Favorable Times of Day:

Ice fishing is most effective during sunrise and sunset when fish are more active and likely to feed.

Additionally, cloudy days can be more productive than sunny ones, as fish tend to feel safer in low-light conditions.

Necessary Equipment:

-Auger: Tool for drilling holes in the ice.
-Rod and Reel: Specialized equipment for ice fishing.
-Ice Fishing Shelter: Portable shelters to protect from wind and cold.
-Fish Finders: Electronic devices to detect fish under the ice.

Ice Fishing Safety:

It is crucial to ensure that the ice is thick enough to support the weight.

A minimum of 10 cm (4 inches) is recommended for a person, and more is required for vehicles.

60

Fishing with Dolphins.

In some regions of Brazil, specifically in the state of Santa Catarina, local fishermen have developed a unique collaboration with wild dolphins to catch fish.

This traditional method, known locally as "pesca com botos," has been practiced for generations and is a fascinating example of cooperation between humans and animals.

The dolphins, usually of the Tursiops type (bottlenose dolphins), work together with the fishermen to primarily catch fish such as mullet (Mugil liza), a species of coastal waters.

The dolphins locate schools of fish and begin to herd them towards the shore.

When the fish are close, the dolphins give a clear signal to the fishermen, such as a strong splash or a specific movement.

The fishermen, attentive to these signals, cast their nets at the spot indicated by the dolphins, catching a large number of fish.

As a reward, the dolphins have access to the fish that escape from the nets or that the fishermen deliberately leave for them.

The arrangement between the fishermen and the dolphins is neither formal nor trained; it is a symbiotic relationship that has evolved naturally.

The dolphins have learned that cooperating with humans results in an easy meal, while the fishermen get a more abundant catch.

This mutually beneficial relationship has endured due to the trust and careful observation of dolphin behaviors by the fishermen.

61

In Greece and other parts of the Mediterranean, octopus fishing is a traditional practice that uses submerged ceramic jars to catch them.

Fishermen use clay pots, known as "octopots," which they place on the seabed.

Octopuses, attracted by the safety of these jars, use them as shelters.

The jars are left in the water for several days or even weeks.

Once it is believed that the jars are occupied, the fishermen return and carefully extract them from the water using ropes tied to the pots.

This technique is employed in various regions of the Mediterranean, including Italy, Spain, and the northern coast of Africa.

This method is sustainable and allows the capture of octopuses without damaging their natural habitat.

62

Fishing with Llamas on Lake Titicaca.

The technique of using llamas for fishing on Lake Titicaca dates back centuries, to pre-Columbian times.

This practice originates from the Andean cultures that have inhabited the region of Lake Titicaca, the highest navigable lake in the world, located between Bolivia and Peru.

The terrain around Lake Titicaca is rugged and difficult to navigate.

Llamas, resilient animals well-adapted to the heights of the Andes, are used to transport fishing nets and other equipment along the shores of the lake.

These regions are inaccessible to modern vehicles and other means of transport, making llamas ideal for this task.

Fishermen load the llamas with nets and fishing gear.

They then guide them along the challenging paths surrounding the lake to the fishing spots.

Once at the location, the nets are deployed in the water to catch fish.

In Lake Titicaca, fishermen primarily catch native species such as suche and carachi, as well as rainbow trout, which was introduced to the lake.

These species are important both for local consumption and for trade.

Fishing with llamas is an integral part of life in the communities around Lake Titicaca.

This practice not only sustains local families by providing food and generating income but also forms part of the rich cultural heritage of the Andean region.

63

The world record for the longest continuous fishing time is 24 hours and 45 minutes, set by Jeff Kolodzinski in 2011.

During this fishing marathon, Kolodzinski demonstrated extraordinary endurance and dedication, fishing non-stop.

This type of record not only requires fishing skills but also a great ability to endure the physical and mental effort of continuous activity.

Kolodzinski, known as the "Marathon Man of Fishing," managed to catch 2,649 fish during this period, highlighting both his skill and perseverance.

Jeff Kolodzinski is a professional fisherman and ambassador of sport fishing, known for his efforts in promoting fishing and the conservation of aquatic resources.

This record was set during a charity event, which also underscores his commitment to social and community causes.

64

Bowfishing.

Bowfishing is a popular practice in some parts of North America, especially in areas with clear, shallow waters such as lakes, rivers, and streams.

In this technique, fishermen use bows and arrows specifically designed for fishing.

The arrow is equipped with a special tip and a fishing line attached to retrieve the fish once it has been hit.

The bows used in bowfishing are similar to hunting bows but often have additional features such as fishing reels to facilitate arrow retrieval.

These arrows are heavier and made of durable materials like fiberglass.

They have special tips with hooks or barbs to ensure the fish does not come loose.

A fishing reel is mounted on the bow, allowing the fisherman to retrieve the arrow and the fish.

The fishing line is robust and designed to withstand the weight and struggle of the fish.

Fishermen shoot the arrows from the shore or a boat, aiming at the visible fish in the water.

Good visibility of the water and the fish is crucial to increase accuracy.

This type of fishing is typically done in shallow waters where the fish can be clearly seen from the surface.

Bowfishing is effective for capturing shallow water fish species such as carp, catfish, tilapia, and gar.

These species often inhabit areas where water visibility is good, allowing fishermen to aim accurately.

It provides a dynamic and exciting fishing experience and allows for the selective control of invasive species like carp.

However, it requires precise archery skills and a keen eye, and it can be challenging in murky or low-visibility waters.

65

Sport Fishing Tournaments

1. Bassmaster Classic:
-Location: United States.
-Description: Known as the "Super Bowl" of sport fishing, the Bassmaster Classic is one of the most prestigious tournaments in the world.
-Prizes: Cash prizes can exceed $300,000 for the winner, with total prizes often surpassing one million dollars.

2. International Game Fish Association (IGFA) World Championship:
-Location: Various locations around the world.
-Description: This tournament attracts the best anglers worldwide who seek to establish new world records.
-Prizes: Varies by event and location but includes cash prizes, trophies, and international recognition.

3. White Marlin Open:
-Location: Ocean City, Maryland, USA.
-Description: The largest white marlin tournament in the world, attracting hundreds of boats each year.
-Prizes: In 2020, the grand prize exceeded $1.9 million dollars.

4. Big Rock Blue Marlin Tournament:
-Location: Morehead City, North Carolina, USA.
-Description: One of the oldest and most prestigious marlin fishing tournaments in the United States.
-Prizes: The total cash prizes can exceed $3 million dollars, with individual prizes of over $1 million.

5. Tuna Tournament:
-Location: Prince Edward Island, Canada.
-Description: Famous for giant tuna fishing, this tournament attracts anglers from all over the world.
-Prizes: Prizes vary but can include large cash sums and high-value fishing gear.

66

Shark Fishing from a Kayak.

Shark fishing from a kayak is especially popular in the coastal regions of Florida, California, Texas, and the east coast of Australia.

These areas offer access to a wide variety of shark species and suitable conditions for kayak fishing.

Commonly caught species include hammerhead shark, bull shark, lemon shark, tiger shark, and blue shark.

Anglers typically use a variety of natural baits such as whole fish (bonito, mackerel), squid, small rays, and oily fish chunks.

Robust rods and high-capacity reels are used to handle the strong pulls from sharks, along with braided lines and steel leaders to prevent the sharks from cutting the line with their teeth.

Fishermen carry first aid kits, personal flotation devices, and often a knife to quickly cut the line in case of an emergency.

They anchor their kayaks near reefs or in deep waters, cast the bait, and wait for a bite.

Once a shark bites, an intense struggle ensues to secure it and then safely release it.

One of the most well-known figures in the realm of shark fishing from a kayak is Robert Field, a fisherman and YouTuber who has extensively documented his adventures and techniques on his YouTube channel "Field Trips with Robert Field."

He has successfully caught numerous shark species and shared his knowledge about kayak fishing through his educational videos.

67

Water Ski Fishing.

Water ski fishing is an extreme and thrilling activity that combines the speed of water skiing with sport fishing.

Fishermen hold onto a boat while being towed at high speed, casting fishing lines and waiting to catch fish.

This form of fishing is practiced in various parts of the world, particularly in lakes and rivers in the United States, Australia, and some coastal areas of Europe.

Fishermen use standard water skis and a sturdy fishing line capable of withstanding the speed and force of a large fish.

Robust rods and high-capacity reels are essential to handle the catch while in motion, and fishermen often use harnesses to securely attach themselves to the boat while casting their lines.

Commonly caught species include walleye, rainbow trout, yellow perch, and pike.

The bait used can vary depending on the target species, but generally includes live bait fish such as minnows and sardines, and artificial lures such as spoons, jigs, and crankbaits designed to attract fish at high speeds.

68

Fishing in Extinct Volcanoes.

Fishing in extinct volcanoes is an exciting activity that takes place in a unique and astonishing environment.

In Mexico, there are two notable locations for this practice: the Arareco Crater in the Sierra Tarahumara, Chihuahua, and the Alchichica Crater, also known as the Laguna de Alchichica, in Puebla.

These locations offer the opportunity to fish for trout in crystal-clear waters surrounded by an impressive volcanic landscape.

Fishermen use standard fishing techniques, such as fly fishing or lure fishing, adapted to the crater environment.

Common equipment like fishing rods, reels, lines, and lures are used according to individual preferences and the species targeted.

In these bodies of water, trout is commonly found, although depending on the location and characteristics of the site, other species such as catfish and whitefish can also be encountered.

The bait used varies according to the target species and the fisherman's preferences, with natural baits like worms, insects, or small fish being common.

69

**In modern sport fishing, the use of drones
is revolutionizing how anglers approach their prey.**

This advanced technology allows them to locate schools of fish from the air and drop lures or baits in precise locations, opening up new possibilities and exciting challenges.

One place where this technique is being used is the Great Lakes of North America, such as Lake Michigan and Lake Erie.

Here, fishermen use drones to explore vast expanses of water and locate schools of fish in remote areas.

Drone fishing involves flying the device over the water and using a camera mounted on the drone to look for signs of fish activity, such as movements on the water's surface or clusters of seabirds indicating the presence of fish near the surface.

The tools used in this form of fishing primarily include drones equipped with high-resolution cameras and GPS navigation systems to perform precise and stable flights over the water.

Additionally, fishermen need standard fishing gear, such as rods and reels, to drop lures or baits from the drone into the water.

The types of fish that can be caught using this technique depend on the specific fishing area but can include species such as pike, salmon, bass, and trout, among others.

Characteristics of Drones Used for Sport Fishing:

-High-Resolution Camera: Equipped with high-resolution cameras that allow fishermen to clearly see the water from the air. This enables them to spot schools of fish, identify the location of prey, and track their activity from an elevated perspective.

-Bait Release Systems: Some drones are designed with built-in bait release systems that allow fishermen to transport and drop lures or bait in precise locations in the water. These drones often have arms or hooks that can hold the bait and release it when they are over the desired fishing area.

-GPS Navigation: Drones with integrated GPS navigation are especially useful for sport fishing, as they allow fishermen to program precise flight routes and keep the drone stationary over a specific area for extended periods. This is crucial for maintaining a clear view of the water and making accurate bait drops.

-Water-Resistant: Some drones are specifically designed to withstand water splashes and adverse weather conditions, making them ideal for sport fishing in aquatic environments. These drones typically have waterproof casings and sealed electronic components to protect them from water.

70

Sharks Capable of Adapting
to Both Fresh and Salt Water.

Although most sharks are marine and need saltwater
to survive, some species can migrate to freshwater
environments and adjust to living in them temporarily.

Among these species, the bull shark (Carcharhinus leucas)
stands out for its ability to tolerate a wide range of salinities.

They are found in rivers, lakes, estuaries, and coastal areas
worldwide, being one of the few euryhaline species.

Additionally, the river shark (Glyphis garricki) is a freshwater
species limited to rivers and estuaries in Australia, though it is
critically endangered due to human activities.

These sharks can be found in tropical and subtropical areas
on different continents, from the southern United States to
Australia.

In terms of diet, they are opportunistic predators that feed
on fish, crustaceans, cephalopods, and marine mammals,
adapting their diet according to their environment.

To survive in environments with different salinities, these
sharks have developed notable physiological adaptations.

These include osmoregulation, which allows them to regulate
the concentration of salts in their bodies to adapt to the
surrounding water.

They also have a high tolerance for osmotic stress and can
travel long distances between fresh and saltwater to take
advantage of a variety of habitats and food resources.

Fishing and Baits

Learn to make simple and economical homemade recipes that will allow you to create highly effective fishing baits adapted to both freshwater and saltwater species that you wish to catch.

Made in the USA
Monee, IL
26 November 2024

71291258R00063